THE

3•MINUTE

refresh

DEVOTIONAL

FOR WOMEN

THE

3 • MINUTE

refresh

DEVOTIONAL

FOR WOMEN

365 Bible Readings

to Inspire Your Heart

BARBOUR
PUBLISHING

ISBN 978-1-63609-988-0

Cover Design by Greg Jackson, Thinkpen Design

Published by Barbour Publishing, Inc., 1810 Barbour Drive, Uhrichsville, Ohio 44683, www.barbourbooks.com

Our mission is to inspire the world with the life-changing message of the Bible.

Member of the
Evangelical Christian
Publishers Association

Printed in China.

[The Lord] lets me rest in green meadows;
he leads me beside peaceful streams.
He renews my strength. He guides me along
right paths, bringing honor to his name.

PSALM 23:2–3 NLT

INTRODUCTION
3 Minutes to Refresh Your Lovely Soul

These devotions were written especially for those moments when you need a little reminder that your heavenly Father offers you renewal and rest—today and every day. Just three short minutes will help to comfort and encourage your spirit as He works to do a new work in you.

- ◗ Minute 1: Read the day's Bible verse and reflect on its meaning.

- ◗ Minute 2: Read the devotional and think about its application to your life.

- ◗ Minute 3: Pray.

Although these devotions aren't meant as a tool for deep Bible study, they can be a touch point to keep you rooted in and focused on God, who listens to your every prayer. May every moment you spend with this book be a blessing!

DAY 1
Gratitude Bookends

They are to stand every morning to thank and to praise the LORD, and likewise at evening.
1 CHRONICLES 23:30 NASB

Here's a good practice for us all: begin each day by saying thank You to the Lord, and end each day by doing the same. That way, our days are bookended by gratitude. It's a great way to start the day, one that will bring hope and energy to our mornings; and it's also a wonderful way to end the day, refocusing our minds on positive things so that we can settle down peacefully to sleep. Try it for the next week. As soon as you wake up, say something as short and simple as, "Thank You, Lord," and then when you get into bed, repeat the same words. See if it changes the way you feel about life.

Lord, may each of my days begin and end with thanksgiving. Amen.

DAY 2
Joy in the Morning

All who seek the LORD will praise him.
Their hearts will rejoice with everlasting joy.
PSALM 22:26 NLT

Every day, God provides us with beauty all around to cheer and help us. It may come through the beauty of flowers or the bright blue sky—or maybe the white snow covering the trees of a glorious winter wonderland. It may be through the smile of a child or the grateful face of the one we care for. Each and every day, the Lord has a special gift to remind us of whose we are and to generate the joy we need to succeed.

Lord God, I thank You for Your joy; I thank
You for providing it every day to sustain
me. I will be joyful in You. Amen.

DAY 3
Completion

When it came time for the dedication of the wall, they tracked down and brought in the Levites from all their homes in Jerusalem to carry out the dedication with exuberance: thanksgiving hymns, songs, cymbals, harps, and lutes.
NEHEMIAH 12:27 MSG

During the time that God's people lived in exile, the city of Jerusalem had fallen into ruins. When Nehemiah heard the news, he felt called by God to go back to Jerusalem and rebuild the wall around the city. It was a huge task that involved overcoming political opposition as well as putting in days of careful planning followed by hard, sweaty labor. When the wall was completed, Nehemiah must have felt a huge sense of satisfaction— but instead of allowing his pride to turn into an ego trip, he immediately dedicated his work to God. He turned the completion of this immense project into an opportunity for an exuberant celebration of thanksgiving.

Remind me, Lord, to dedicate each project I undertake to You. Amen.

DAY 4
Alertness

*Devote yourselves to prayer, keeping alert in
it with an attitude of thanksgiving.*
Colossians 4:2 nasb

Jesus promised us that His yoke is easy, not heavy to
carry (Matthew 11:30), and that the life of a Christian
is not meant to be hard. That doesn't mean, though, that
we can get careless and sloppy about our calling to be
people of God. If we do, we will all too easily slip back
into worry, resentment, gossiping, complaining, overin-
dulgence, and all sorts of other unhealthy and unloving
practices. The Bible reminds us to stay alert—to pay
attention and be careful that we are staying close to
God in our hearts and lives. How do we do that? By
praying daily and constantly maintaining an attitude
of thanksgiving.

---

*I want to stay alert, Lord, so remind me that I can't
afford to stop praying or practicing gratitude. Amen.*

DAY 5
God's Command

So He said, "Come." And when Peter had come down out of the boat, he walked on the water to go to Jesus.
MATTHEW 14:29 NKJV

Jesus stayed behind to send the crowds away—and then to pray. Later that evening, the disciples, wrestling their boat against a contrary wind, saw a ghostly figure approaching. Jesus assured them it was He, and Peter asked the Lord to command him to come. Jesus did—and Peter, briefly, walked on water. What does it take for an ordinary person to walk on water? A command of God. By the power of God, ordinary men and women, responding to God's call, have successfully accomplished difficult, even impossible, tasks.

You are my strength, O Lord. Whenever I feel like giving up, I will turn to You, believing that You will give me the power to carry on. Amen.

DAY 6
Loyal Hearts

"For the eyes of the LORD range throughout the earth to strengthen those whose hearts are fully committed to him."
2 CHRONICLES 16:9 NIV

God seeks a relationship with those who have open and receiving hearts. He is not looking to condemn or judge but to find hearts committed to knowing Him and learning His way. He desires people who want to talk and listen to Him and who have a deep thirst to serve and please Him. God looks for us, and the only requirement is for each of us to have a fully devoted heart. We open our hearts and hands to receive Him, and He will find us.

Find me, Lord; draw me near to You.
Open up my heart so that I may fully receive
all that You want to pour into it. Amen.

DAY 7
He Enjoys You

*"The LORD your God is living among you. He is
a mighty savior. He will take delight in you with
gladness. With his love, he will calm all your fears.
He will rejoice over you with joyful songs."*
ZEPHANIAH 3:17 NLT

Zephaniah's words remind us that God is our loving
parent. Our mighty Savior offers us a personal relationship, loving and rejoicing over us, His children, glad that
we live and move in Him. He is the Lord of the universe,
and yet He will quiet our restless hearts and minds with
His tender love. He delights in our lives and celebrates
our union with Him. We can rest in His affirmation
and love, no matter what circumstances surround us.

---

*Lord, help me remember that You are always with
me and that You delight in me. Remind me that I am
Your child and that You enjoy our relationship. Amen.*

DAY 8
Shine On!

Let the message about Christ, in all its richness,
fill your lives. Teach and counsel each other with
all the wisdom he gives. Sing psalms and hymns
and spiritual songs to God with thankful hearts.
COLOSSIANS 3:16 NLT

We need to live the Word of God every day. It will shine through us! A famous song says, "They'll know we are Christians by our love." This means reflecting the love of God in everything we do. When we spend time in God's Word, we find peace, wisdom, and contentment that we get from no other place. This is a peace we love to have. This is happiness! Imagine being anything but thankful to God for filling us with His love, peace, and wisdom!

Oh Lord, my Rock and my Redeemer, may my
words and my actions be a reflection of Your
Word and pleasing in Your sight. Amen.

DAY 9
Unshakable

Therefore, since we receive a kingdom which cannot be shaken, let's show gratitude, by which we may offer to God an acceptable service with reverence and awe.

HEBREWS 12:28 NASB

Our emotions go up and down. Even within a single day, we may shift from joy to sorrow, from laughter to anger. Emotions are a normal and healthy part of being human, but we don't need to let them rule our lives. Gratitude can be the steady thread that keeps us tied firmly to the kingdom of God, a reality that never changes. In the midst of each feeling we experience, a sense of thankfulness will keep us from shaking. At times we may struggle to feel thankful, but as we consciously practice our awareness of God's presence, gratitude will become a habit that holds us steady through all our emotions.

Oh God of power and might, may I never lose sight of Your amazing reality. May my gratitude to You be the underlying bedrock of all I feel. Amen.

Good

For everything created by God is good, and nothing is to be rejected if it is received with gratitude.
1 TIMOTHY 4:4 NASB

When God created the world, He declared that each thing He made was good. Too often, however, we human beings have abused or misused the good things God created. We overindulge in ways that harm both our bodies and creation. Or we swing the other way and erect rules and boundaries around certain things, denying ourselves for no good reason. The Bible gives us a middle road between these two extremes. When gratitude becomes the light in which we live, we will find ourselves able to live in moderation, accepting God's goodness without selfishness or greed.

Loving Lord, thank You for Your wonderful creation. Teach me to honor it. May each thing I do, whether it's eating, driving my car, or buying clothes, be to Your glory. Amen.

The Lord Himself Goes before You

"The LORD himself goes before you and will be with you; he will never leave you nor forsake you. Do not be afraid; do not be discouraged."
DEUTERONOMY 31:8 NIV

Joshua 1:9 tells us to "be strong and courageous. Do not be afraid; do not be discouraged, for the LORD your God will be with you wherever you go." Be encouraged! Even when it feels like it, you are truly never alone, and never without access to God's power. If you've trusted Christ as your Savior, the Spirit of God Himself is alive and well and working inside you at all times. What an astounding miracle! The Creator of the universe dwells within you and is available to encourage you and help you make right choices on a moment-by-moment basis.

Thank You, Lord, for the incredible gift of Your presence in each and every situation I face. Allow me to remember this and to call upon Your name as I go about each day. Amen.

DAY 12
God of Possible

Jesus looked at them and said, "With man this is impossible, but with God all things are possible."
MATTHEW 19:26 NIV

No one can be saved by her own efforts! Man's greatest efforts pale in comparison to the requirements of a holy God. But grace, freely offered by God and accepted by individuals, will admit us to heaven. With God, all things *are* possible—especially enabling forgiven sinners to live eternally. Realizing we can do nothing is the key to gaining everything.

Dear Father, I appreciate Your grace—
Your loving-kindness that I don't deserve.
There is nothing I have done to earn it. Grace
is Your gift to me, and I thank You. Amen.

DAY 13
Visible Reminders

Let the morning bring me word of your unfailing love, for I have put my trust in you.
PSALM 143:8 NIV

We don't know if David was a morning person or a night owl, but he chose to start his day looking for visible reminders of God's unfailing love. It might have been easy to remember God's love for him if he had witnessed a glorious morning sunrise, but if the night had been stormy and he was dealing with spooked sheep in the midst of a downpour, God's unfailing love may have felt a little distant. Whether or not conditions were favorable for faith, David believed in God's unfailing love—even if he couldn't see it in the world around him.

I awake in the morning, and You are there. You are with me all day long and throughout the night. Thank You, heavenly Father, for Your ever-present love. Amen.

Sweet Aroma

*The heartfelt counsel of a friend is as
sweet as perfume and incense.*
PROVERBS 27:9 NLT

Whether it's over coffee, dessert, or even on the phone,
a cherished friend can offer the encouragement and
God-directed counsel we all need from time to time.
Friendships that have Christ as their center are wonderful relationships blessed by the Father. Through the
timely, godly advice these friends offer, God speaks to
us, showering us with comfort that is as sweet as perfume and incense. So, what are you waiting for? Make
a date with a friend and share the sweet aroma of Jesus!

---

*Jesus, Your friendship means the world to me.
I value the close friendships You've blessed me
with too! Thank You for the special women in
my life. Show me every day how to be a blessing
to them, just as they are to me. Amen.*

DAY 15
Every Step of the Way

Never stop praying.
1 THESSALONIANS 5:17 NLT

God wants to be involved in our daily routines. He wants to hear from us and waits for us. God never promised an easy life to Christians. If we will allow Him, though, God will be there with us every step of the way. All we need to do is come to Him in prayer. With these three simple words from 1 Thessalonians 5:17, our lives can be fulfilling as we live to communicate with our Lord.

Father, when I pray, remind me that prayer is not only about talking to You, but also about listening to You. Open my heart to Your words. Amen.

Get Above It All

*Set your affection on things above,
not on things on the earth.*
COLOSSIANS 3:2 KJV

Sometimes the most difficult challenges you face play out in your head—where a struggle to control the outcome and work out the details of life can consume you. Once removed—far away from the details—you can see things from a higher perspective. Close your eyes and push out the thoughts that try to grab you and keep you tied to the things of the world. Reach out to God and let your spirit soar. Give your concerns to Him and let Him work out the details. Rest in Him and He'll carry you above it all, every step of the way.

God, You are far above any detail of life that concerns me. Help me to trust You today for answers to those things that seem to bring me down. I purposefully set my heart and mind on You today. Amen.

DAY 17
Promises of God

"For the LORD your God is living among you.
He is a mighty savior. He will take delight in you
with gladness. With his love, he will calm all your
fears. He will rejoice over you with joyful songs."
ZEPHANIAH 3:17 NLT

Look at all the promises packed into this one verse of scripture! God is with you. He is your mighty savior. He delights in you with gladness. He calms your fears with His love. He rejoices over you with joyful songs. Wow! What a bundle of hope is found here for the believer. Like a mother attuned to her newborn baby's cries, so is your heavenly Father's heart for you. He delights in being your Father. You are blessed to be a daughter of the King.

Father, thank You for loving me the way
You do. You are all I need. Amen.

DAY 18
Soul Comfort

*In the multitude of my anxieties within
me, Your comforts delight my soul.*
PSALM 94:19 NKJV

We don't know for sure who wrote Psalm 94, but we can
be certain that the psalmist was annoyed and anxious
when he wrote it. He cries out to God, asking Him to
"pay back to the proud what they deserve" (v. 2 NIV).
Then, he goes on with a list of accusations about the
evil ones before saying, "In the multitude of my anxieties within me." Does that phrase describe you? When
anxiety overwhelms us, we find relief in the words of
Psalm 94:19. When we turn our anxious thoughts over
to God, He brings contentment to our souls.

---

*Dear God, on those days when frustration and
anxiety overwhelm me, please come to me, comfort
my soul, and remind me to praise You. Amen.*

DAY 19

The New Me

*Therefore, if anyone is in Christ, the new creation
has come: The old has gone, the new is here!*
2 CORINTHIANS 5:17 NIV

Are you in Christ? Is He consistently Lord of your life?
Then you are a new creation. *Everything* is new. What's
history is done and over—and Jesus has replaced your
old with His new: new peace, new joy, new love, new
strength. Since God Himself sees us as a new creation,
how can we do any less? We need to choose to see
ourselves as a new creation too. And we can, through
God's grace. Be glad. Give thanks. Live each day as the
new creation you have become through Jesus.

---

*Father, I'm so thankful that You are a God of grace—
and I thank You that I am a new creation. Please give
me the spiritual eyes to see myself as a new creation,
looking past the guilt of yesterday's choices. Amen.*

DAY 20
He First Loved Us

*This is how God showed his love among
us: He sent his one and only Son into the
world that we might live through him.*

1 JOHN 4:9 NIV

Many things about God are quite a mystery. If there is
anything at all that we can understand for sure, though,
we can know He loves us. There is nothing we could
ever do to make God *stop* loving us, because certainly
we did nothing to make Him start. God is concerned
about everything we do. He celebrates our victories and
cries with us during our difficult times. God proved His
love for us long before we were ever born! How could
we not love such a God who first loved us so much?

---

*You have always loved me, God, and You will love me
forever. I am so grateful! Compared to Yours, my love
is small, but I love You with all of my heart. Amen.*

Planted Deep

*Fix these words of mine in your hearts and
minds; tie them as symbols on your hands
and bind them on your foreheads.*
DEUTERONOMY 11:18 NIV

Memorizing Bible verses isn't a fashionable trend in today's world, but learning key verses plants the Word of God deeply in our hearts. We draw strength and nourishment in dark times from remembering what God told us in the Bible. In times of crisis, we recall God's promises of hope and comfort. In our everyday moments, repeating well-known verses reminds us that God is always with us—whether it feels like it or not.

---

*What an awesome gift You have given me, God—
the Bible! I will fix Your words in my mind and heart
and carry them with me wherever I go. Amen.*

DAY 22
Chosen

"I have chosen you and have not rejected you."
ISAIAH 41:9 NIV

The Lord doesn't dump us when we don't measure up. And He doesn't choose us one minute only to reject us a week later. We need not fear being deserted by our loving Father. He doesn't accept or reject us based on any arbitrary standards. He loves us with an everlasting love (Jeremiah 31:3). By His own mercy and design, "he hath made us accepted in the beloved" (Ephesians 1:6 KJV).

---

*Father, thank You that I don't need to
fear Your rejection of me. Amen.*

Never Forgotten

The Lord will keep you from all harm—he will watch over your life; the Lord will watch over your coming and going both now and forevermore.
Psalm 121:7–8 NIV

Our lives are like an ancient city contained within walls. In an ancient city, the gatekeeper's job was to make decisions about what went in and out of the city. God is the gatekeeper of our lives. He is always watching, always guarding, and ever vigilant in His care of us—even when we are least aware that He is doing so. Proverbs 2:8 (NKJV) says, "He guards the paths of justice, and preserves the way of His saints." By sending His Son to save us and His Spirit to dwell in us, He has assured us that we are never forgotten and never alone.

Forgive me, Father, for how often I forget about You. Help me remember that You are guarding and preserving me and that nothing comes into my life without Your permission. Amen.

DAY 24
Object of Faith

And as Moses lifted up the serpent in the wilderness,
even so must the Son of Man be lifted up, that whoever
believes in Him should not perish but have eternal life.
JOHN 3:14–15 NKJV

When Nicodemus inquires of Jesus how a man receives
eternal life, Jesus recalls this Old Testament image.
Knowing He would be lifted up on a cross, the Lord
Jesus points Nicodemus and us to faith in Him alone.
We must repent of our sin and believe in the Son of
God who died on the cross. Sin and its consequences
are around us like serpents, but into the midst of our
fallen world, God has sent Jesus to save us. He is the
object of our faith. The crucified and resurrected Christ
is the answer. He is the truth, the way, and the life.

Father, fix my gaze on Your Son lifted up for me. Amen.

DAY 25
Secure in Truth

Throw off your old sinful nature and your former
way of life, which is corrupted by lust and deception.
Instead, let the Spirit renew your thoughts and
attitudes. Put on your new nature, created to
be like God—truly righteous and holy.
EPHESIANS 4:22–24 NLT

In Christ, we have a new mindset—fresh thinking. We know we are loved and treasured. The very God who spoke the universe into existence loved us enough to leave heaven and live in this imperfect world so He could save us from eternity in the hell we so deserved. Talk about significance! The delusions of this world fall away in light of who He is and what He has done for love of us. Our daily intake of His Word secures us in those truths. The lies of the evil one become ineffective.

Christ, rid me of my old way of thinking.
Put the new mindset within me to see daily the
lies I fall for. Help me to walk in rightness and
holiness, reflecting You in all I am. Amen.

DAY 26
Unchained!

*The Spirit you received does not make you slaves,
so that you live in fear again; rather, the Spirit
you received brought about your adoption to
sonship. And by him we cry, "Abba, Father."*
ROMANS 8:15 NIV

Do you struggle with fear? Do you feel it binding you
with its invisible chains? If so, then there's good news.
Through Jesus, you have received the Spirit of sonship.
A son (or daughter) of the most high God has nothing
to fear. Knowing you've been set free is enough to make
you cry, "Abba, Father!" in praise. Today, acknowledge
your fears to the Lord. He will loose your chains and
set you free.

---

*Lord, thank You that You are the great chain breaker!
I don't have to live in fear. I am Your child, Your
daughter, and You are my Daddy-God! Amen.*

DAY 27
Not Withholding

Anything I wanted, I would take. I denied myself no pleasure. I even found great pleasure in hard work, a reward for all my labors.
ECCLESIASTES 2:10 NLT

Work beckons. Deadlines loom. You're trying to balance your home life against your work life, and it's overwhelming. Take heart! It is possible to rejoice in your labors—to find pleasure in the day-to-day tasks. At work or at play. . .let the Lord cause a song of joy to rise up in your heart.

Help me to slow down—every day—and enjoy the moments as they come, Father God. May I not become so busy that I miss out on life's simple pleasures. Amen.

DAY 28
Standing Firm

I. . .didn't dodge their insults, faced them as they spit in my face. And the Master, God, stays right there and helps me, so I'm not disgraced. Therefore I set my face like flint, confident that I'll never regret this. My champion is right here. Let's take our stand together!
ISAIAH 50:6–8 MSG

Isaiah reminds us that we are not alone in our battles—even when everyone is against us and we feel outnumbered and outmaneuvered. But remember, your champion, God, is right there, saying, "I am not leaving you! We are sticking this out together. You can put your chin up confidently, knowing that I, the sustainer, am on your side. Let's take our stand together!"

Lord, boldly stand beside me. May the strength of Your arms gird me as I take a stand for You. Lift my chin today; give me confidence to face opposition, knowing You are right there with me. Amen.

DAY 29
Holding the Line

When I said, "My foot is slipping," your unfailing love, LORD, supported me. When anxiety was great within me, your consolation brought me joy.
PSALM 94:18–19 NIV

Often we may feel that our feet are slipping in life. We lose our grip. Anxiety becomes a sleep-robber, headache-giver, and joy-squelcher. Fear takes over our hearts. All we can think is, *Just get me out of here!* But we must remember who is anchoring our life. God's powerful grip secures us—even in the most difficult times. He comforts us with His loving presence that defies understanding. He provides wisdom to guide our steps through life's toughest challenges. We can rest assured that His support is steady, reliable, and motivated by His love for us.

Jesus, my rock and fortress, thank You that Your strength is made available to me. Steady me with the surety of Your love. Replace my anxiety with peace and joy, reflecting a life that's secured by the Almighty. Amen.

Revel in the Beauty

He has made everything beautiful in its time. He has also set eternity in the human heart; yet no one can fathom what God has done from beginning to end.
ECCLESIASTES 3:11 NIV

No one can completely "fathom what God has done." That's what makes Him God. And yet, still we try. Thankfully, our hearts don't need to understand; neither do they need earthly "fixes." They just need to be set free, to find God and revel in the beauty of His never-ending creation. Believers, stop letting unanswerable questions prevent you from loving Him more completely. And unbelievers, ask yourself, if you had every material thing you could want, wouldn't your heart still be reaching out for eternity?

I have questions, God—so many unanswered questions about life and about You. Increase my trust in You. Help me to set aside my uncertainty and to delight in Your never-ending love. Amen.

DAY 31
Joy in Your Work

*Go, eat your food with gladness, and drink
your wine with a joyful heart, for God
has already approved what you do.*
ECCLESIASTES 9:7 NIV

Ever feel like nothing you do is good enough? Your boss
is frustrated over something you've done wrong. The
kids are complaining. Your neighbors are even upset
at you. How wonderful to read that God accepts our
works, even when we feel lacking. He encourages us to
go our way with a merry heart, completely confident
that we are accepted in the Beloved.

---

*When it feels like I'm a complete failure—
and that I am letting others down, Lord—please
infuse my soul with confidence. No matter what,
I am Yours. I am accepted. I am loved. Amen.*

People Pleaser vs. God Pleaser

*We are not trying to please people
but God, who tests our hearts.*
1 THESSALONIANS 2:4 NIV

When we allow ourselves to be real before God, it doesn't matter what others think. If the God of the universe has accepted us, then who cares about someone else's opinion? It is impossible to please both God and man. We must make a choice. Man looks at the outward appearance, but God looks at the heart. Align your heart with His. Let go of impression management that focuses on outward appearance. Receive God's unconditional love, and enjoy the freedom to be yourself before Him!

Dear Lord, may I live for You alone. Help me transition from a people pleaser to a God pleaser. Amen.

A Net of Love

No one has ever seen God; but if we love one another,
God lives in us and his love is made complete in us.

1 JOHN 4:12 NIV

It's hard to be a good witness if you've got a sour expression on your face. People aren't usually won to the Lord by grumpy friends and coworkers. If you hope to persuade people that life in Jesus is the ultimate, then you've got to let your enthusiasm shine through. Before you reach for the net, spend some time on your knees asking for an infusion of joy. Then, go catch some fish!

Dear heavenly Father, I want to be a good witness
for You. Help me remember to exude joy and love
so that others will be drawn to You. Amen.

DAY 34
Faith and Action

And I keep praying that this faith we hold in common keeps showing up in the good things we do, and that people recognize Christ in all of it.
PHILEMON 1:6 MSG

Our actions and reactions are a powerful gauge of how serious we are about our faith. When others wrong us, do we refuse to forgive and risk misrepresenting Christ? Or do we freely offer forgiveness as an expression of our faith? God calls us to faith and forgiveness in Christ Jesus so that Christians and non-Christians alike will see our good deeds and praise God.

Dear Lord, please let me remember that people look to me for a glimpse of You. Let my actions always reflect my faith in You. Amen.

Living a Complete Life

It is a good thing to receive wealth from God and the good health to enjoy it.
ECCLESIASTES 5:19 NLT

God has promised to supply all your needs, but it takes action on your part. Seeking wisdom for your situation and asking God to direct you in the right decisions will help you find a well-balanced life that will produce success, coupled with the health to enjoy it. It may be as simple as realizing a vacation is exactly what you need instead of working throughout the year and taking your vacation in cash to pay for new bedroom furniture. Know when to press forward and when to stop and enjoy the life God has given you for His good pleasure—and yours!

Lord, I ask for Your wisdom to help me balance my life so I can be complete in every area of my life. Amen.

He Will Send Help

"The waves of death swirled about me; the torrents of destruction overwhelmed me. . . . In my distress I called to the LORD. . . . From his temple he heard my voice; my cry came to his ears."

2 SAMUEL 22:5, 7 NIV

God never asked us to do life alone. When the waves of death swirl around us, and the pounding rain of destruction threatens to overwhelm us, we can cry out to our heavenly Father, knowing that He will not let us drown. He will hear our voice, and He will send help. So, next time you feel that you can't put one foot in front of the other, ask God to send you His strength and energy. He will help you to live out your purpose in this chaotic world.

Lord, thank You for strengthening me when the "dailyness" of life, and its various trials, threatens to overwhelm me. Amen.

God as He Really Is

*The Lord is compassionate and gracious, slow to anger,
abounding in love. . . . He does not treat us as our
sins deserve or repay us according to our iniquities.*
PSALM 103:8, 10 NIV

Our attitude toward God can influence the way we
handle what He has given us. Some people perceive
God as a harsh and angry judge, impatiently tapping
His foot, saying, "When will you ever get it right?"
People who see God this way can become paralyzed by
an unhealthy fear of Him. However, the Bible paints
a very different picture of God. Psalm 103 says He is
gracious and compassionate, that He does not treat
us as our sins deserve. What difference can it make in
your life to know that you serve a loving God who is
longing to be gracious to you?

*Lord, thank You for Your compassion,
Your grace, and Your mercy. Help me to
see You as You really are. Amen.*

DAY 38

Changing Our Perspective

Turn my eyes away from worthless things;
preserve my life according to your word.
PSALM 119:37 NIV

The book of Psalms offers hundreds of verses that can easily become sentence prayers. "Turn my eyes away from worthless things" whispered before heading out to shop, turning on the television, or picking up a magazine can turn those experiences into opportunities to see God's hand at work in our lives. He can change our perspective. He will show us what has value for us. He can even change our appetites, causing us to desire the very things He wants for us. When we pray this prayer, we are asking God to show us what He wants for us. He knows us and loves us more than we know and love ourselves. We can trust His love and goodness to provide for our needs.

Father, help me remember to pray this prayer
and to relinquish my desires to You. Amen.

Keep Smiling

*"When they were discouraged, I smiled at them.
My look of approval was precious to them."*
JOB 29:24 NLT

Our most authentic forms of communication occur without a word. Rather, they flow from an understanding smile, a compassionate touch, a loving gesture, a gentle presence, or an unspoken prayer. God used Job, an ordinary man with an extraordinary amount of love and wisdom—a man whose only adornment was righteous living and a warm smile. And He wants to use us too. So, keep smiling. Someone may just need it.

Remind me, Jesus, to bless others through my actions. A warm smile, a simple act of kindness, or a loving touch might be just what someone needs today. Remind me, please. Amen.

The Key to Happiness

He who heeds the word wisely will find good,
and whoever trusts in the LORD, happy is he.

Want the key to true happiness? Try wisdom. When others around you are losing their heads, losing their cool, and losing sleep over their decisions, choose to react differently. Step up to the plate. Handle matters wisely. Wise choices always lead to joyous outcomes. And along the way, you will be setting an example for others around you to follow. So, c'mon. . .get happy! Get wisdom!

Father, thank You for the wisdom of Your Word,
which will always point me in the right direction
when I have a choice to make. Amen.

DAY 41
Shake It Up!

The LORD had said to Abram, "Leave your native country, your relatives, and your father's family, and go to the land that I will show you. . . . I will bless you. . .and you will be a blessing to others."
GENESIS 12:1–2 NLT

In God's wisdom, He likes to shake us up a little, stretch us out of our comfort zone, push us out on a limb. Yet, we resist the change, cling to what's known, and try to change His mind with fat, sloppy tears. Are you facing a big change? God wants us to be willing to embrace change that He brings into our lives. Even unbidden change. You may feel as if you're out on a limb, but don't forget that God is the tree trunk. He's not going to let you fall.

Holy, loving Father, in every area of my life, teach me to trust You more deeply. Amen.

A Royal Vision

Yes, joyful are those who live like this!
Joyful indeed are those whose God is the Lord.
PSALM 144:15 NLT

How wonderful to realize you're God's child. He loves you and wants nothing but good for you. Doesn't knowing you're His daughter send waves of joy through your soul? How happy we are when we recognize that we are princesses—children of the most high God! Listen closely as He whispers royal secrets in your ear. Your heavenly Father offers you keys to the kingdom. . .and vision for the road ahead.

Joy floods my soul when I think about
how much You love me, Lord. Thank You
for making me Your child. Amen.

Spirit and Truth

*"But the time is coming—indeed it's here
now—when true worshipers will worship
the Father in spirit and in truth."*

JOHN 4:23 NLT

God is everywhere all the time, and He doesn't just want
to be worshiped at church. You can worship God on your
way to work, during class, as you clean your house, and
as you pay your bills. Worship is about living your life
in a way that is pleasing to the Lord and seeking Him
first in all things. Paying your bills? Ask God how He
wants you to spend your money. That is pleasing to Him,
and that is worship. In the middle of class? Be respectful
of your professors, and use the brain God gave you to
complete your studies. If you are living your everyday
life to please God, that is worship!

---

*Father, help me to live my life in ways that
please You. Let my focus be on worshiping
You in everything I do. Amen.*

DAY 44
Heavenly Appreciation

*God is not unjust; he will not forget your work
and the love you have shown him as you have
helped his people and continue to help them.*
HEBREWS 6:10 NIV

Sometimes it seems our hard work is ignored. When our work for Christ seems to go unnoticed by our church family, we can be assured that God sees our hard work and appreciates it. We may not receive the "church member of the month" award, but our love for our brothers and sisters in Christ and our work on their behalf is not overlooked by God. The author of Hebrews assures us that God is not unjust—our reward is in heaven.

---

*Dear Lord, You are a God of love and justice.
Even when I do not receive the notice of those around
me, help me to serve You out of my love for You. Amen.*

Release the Music Within

*Those who are wise will find a time
and a way to do what is right.*
ECCLESIASTES 8:5 NLT

It has been said that many people go to their graves with their music still in them. Do you carry a song within your heart, waiting to be heard? Whether we are eight or eighty, it is never too late to surrender our hopes and dreams to God. A wise woman trusts that God will help her find the time and manner in which to use her talents for His glory as she seeks His direction. Let the music begin.

Dear Lord, my music is fading against the constant beat of a busy pace. I surrender my gifts to You and pray for the time and manner in which I can use those gifts to touch my world. Amen.

Enjoying Life

*May all who seek You rejoice and be glad
in You; and may those who love Your
salvation say continually, "May God be
exalted!"...You are my help and my savior.*
PSALM 70:4–5 NASB

Sometimes we approach God robotically: "Lord, please do this for me. Lord, please do that." We're convinced we'll be happy if only God grants our wishes like a genie in a bottle. We're going about this backward! We should start by praising God. Thank Him for life, health, and the many answered prayers. Our joyous praise will remind us just how blessed we already are! Then—out of genuine relationship—we make our requests known.

---

*Father God, my joy comes from You—and only
You. Without You I could never experience all of
the joys that life has to offer. Thank You! Amen.*

DAY 47
He Is Faithful

If we are unfaithful, he remains faithful,
for he cannot deny who he is.
2 TIMOTHY 2:13 NLT

Sometimes we treat our relationship with God the same as we do with other people. We promise Him we'll start spending more time with Him in prayer and Bible study. Soon the daily distractions of life get in the way, and we're back in our same routine, minus prayer and Bible study. Even when we fail to live up to our expectations, our heavenly Father doesn't pick up His judge's gavel and condemn us for unfaithfulness. Instead, He remains a faithful supporter, encouraging us to keep trying to hold up our end of the bargain. Take comfort in His faithfulness, and let that encourage you toward a deeper relationship with Him.

Father, thank You for Your unending faithfulness.
Every day I fall short of Your standards, but You're
always there, encouraging me and lifting me up.
Please help me to be more faithful to You—in
the big things and in the little things. Amen.

DAY 48
Learn Contentment

*I am not saying this because I am in need, for I have
learned to be content whatever the circumstances.*
Philippians 4:11 NIV

Contentment is learned and cultivated. It is an attitude
of the heart. It has nothing to do with material possessions or life's circumstances. It has everything to do
with being in the center of God's will and knowing it.
Contentment means finding rest and peace in God's
presence—nothing more, nothing less. It is trusting
that God will meet all of your needs. May we learn to
say confidently, *The Lord is my shepherd; I shall not want.*
That is the secret of contentment.

---

*Dear Lord, teach me how to be content in You,
knowing that You will provide all that I need. Amen.*

DAY 49

Love Is. . .

And now these three remain: faith, hope and love. But the greatest of these is love.

1 CORINTHIANS 13:13 NIV

Who can deny the power of faith? Throughout history, faith has closed the mouths of lions, opened blind eyes, and saved countless lost souls. And the scriptures note that without it, we cannot please God (Hebrews 11:6). Yet, as wonderful as these qualities are, it is love that God deems the greatest. Love lasts and never fails. It is patient, kind, unselfish, and honest; it never keeps a record of wrongs or delights in evil. In a word, love is God. And there is no one greater.

Father, I strive to love patiently, kindly, unselfishly, and honestly because in doing so, I become more perfect in love and more like You! Amen.

DAY 50
Simply Silly

A cheerful disposition is good for your health.
PROVERBS 17:22 MSG

Imagine the effect we could have on our world today if our countenance reflected the joy of the Lord all the time: at work, at home, at play. Jesus said, "I have told you this so that my joy may be in you and that your joy may be complete" (John 15:11 NIV). Is your cup of joy full? Have you laughed today? Not a small smile, but laughter. Maybe it's time we looked for something to laugh about and tasted joy. Jesus suggested it.

Lord, help me find joy this day. Let me laugh
and give praises to the King. Amen.

Joyous Tomorrow

But if we hope for that we see not,
then do we with patience wait for it.
ROMANS 8:25 KJV

Are you in a "waiting" season? Is your patience being tested to the breaking point? Take heart! You are not alone. Every godly man and woman from biblical times till now went through seasons of waiting on the Lord. Their secret? They hoped for what they could not see. (They never lost their hope!) And they waited patiently. So, as you're waiting, reflect on the biblical giants and realize. . .you're not alone!

Father, thank You for Your Word that gives examples
of others who have walked the same path before
me. Because of You, I know that I am not alone—
today, tomorrow, or any day after that! Amen.

My Future Is in Your Hands

*The LORD says, "I will guide you along the best pathway
for your life. I will advise you and watch over you."*
PSALM 32:8 NLT

Are plans running wild in your head? Remember that
the Lord is watching over you, and He is there to guide
you. He wants you to seek Him out. Don't try to make
your dreams happen all by yourself. Get on your knees
and ask Him to direct your plans each morning. Don't
be afraid to put your future in His hands!

---

*Father, thank You for always being faithful to me.
Continue to watch over me and direct my path. Amen.*

Jumping Hurdles

God's way is perfect. All the LORD's promises prove true.
PSALM 18:30 NLT

Maybe there are times when you just don't think you can take one more disappointment or hurt. That's the perfect time to draw strength from God and His Word. Meditate on encouraging scriptures, or play a song that you know strengthens your heart and mind. Ask God to infuse you with His strength, and you'll find the power to take another step, and another—until you find yourself on the other side of that challenge you're facing today.

God, give me strength each day to face the obstacles I am to overcome. I am thankful that I don't have to face them alone. Amen.

Anxious Anticipations

I am not saying this because I am in need, for I have learned to be content whatever the circumstances.
PHILIPPIANS 4:11 NIV

Have you ever been so eager for the future that you forgot to be thankful for the present day? Humans have a tendency to complain about the problems and irritations of life. It's much less natural to appreciate the good things we have—until they're gone. While it's fine to look forward to the future, let's remember to reflect on all of *today's* blessings—the large and the small—and appreciate all that we do have.

Thank You, Lord, for the beauty of today.
Please remind me when I become preoccupied with
the future and forget to enjoy the present. Amen.

DAY 55
Second Chances

For his anger lasts only a moment, but his favor lasts a lifetime; weeping may stay for the night, but rejoicing comes in the morning.
PSALM 30:5 NIV

Don't you love second chances? New beginnings? If only we could go back and redo some of our past mistakes. . .what better choices we'd make the second time around. Life in Jesus is all about the rebirth experience—the opportunity to start over. Each day is a new day, in fact. And praise God—the sorrows and trials of yesterday are behind us! With each new morning, joy dawns!

I am so glad You allow second chances, Father. Thank You for each new morning that is an opportunity to start over! Amen.

DAY 56
Light in the Dark

The light shines in the darkness,
and the darkness has not overcome it.
JOHN 1:5 NIV

Jesus said in John 12:46 (NIV), "I have come into the world as a light, so that no one who believes in me should stay in darkness." He also promised that He is always with us. Because we have Him, we have light. If we fail to perceive it, if we seem to be living in darkness, perhaps we have turned our backs to the light of His countenance. Maybe we are covering our eyes with the cares of this world. Clouds of sin may be darkening our lives, but He has not left us. He promises us that in following Him, we will not walk in darkness but will have the light of life.

Lord Jesus, show me my blind spots. Where am I
covering my own eyes or walking away from You?
Turn me back to You, the light of life. Amen.

Fear and Dread

What I feared has come upon me;
what I dreaded has happened to me.
JOB 3:25 NIV

Do we have a secret fear or dread? God knew Job's secret fears, but still called him "blameless and upright" (Job 1:8 NIV). God doesn't withhold His love if we harbor unspoken dread. He doesn't love us any less because of secret anxieties. "The LORD is like a father to his children. . . . He remembers we are only dust" (Psalm 103:13–14 NLT). God never condemned Job (and He'll never condemn us) for private fears. He encourages us, as He did Job, to trust Him. He alone retains control over all creation and all circumstances (Job 38–41).

Father, please stay beside me when what
I dread most comes to me. Amen.

DAY 58
God's Heart

*"I will give them an undivided heart and put a
new spirit in them; I will remove from them their
heart of stone and give them a heart of flesh."*
EZEKIEL 11:19 NIV

God is willing to give us an undivided heart—a heart
that is open and ready to see, hear, and love God. This
heart has a single focus: loving God and others with a
tenderness that we know comes from someone beyond
us. The good news is we have already had successful
surgery and our donor heart is within us. We received
our heart transplant when Jesus died for us, creating a
new spirit within us. God's heart changes everything
and re-creates us as new people with living hearts.

*Thank You, Lord, for giving me a new heart, a heart
so perfect in love that it will last me forever. Amen.*

Refreshing Gift

*For we have great joy and consolation in
your love, because the hearts of the saints
have been refreshed by you, brother.*
PHILEMON 1:7 NKJV

Jesus always took the time for those who reached out
to Him. In a crowd of people, He stopped to help a
woman who touched Him. His quiet love extended to
everyone who asked, whether verbally or with unspoken need. God brings people into our path who need
our encouragement. We must consider those around
us. Smile and thank the waiter, the cashier, the people
who help in small ways. Cheering others can have the
effect of an energizing drink of water so that they will
be able to finish the race with a smile.

---

*Jesus, thank You for being an example of how to
encourage and refresh others. Help me to see their
need and to be willing to reach out. Amen.*

DAY 60
Go Out with Joy

*For ye shall go out with joy, and be led forth
with peace: the mountains and the hills shall
break forth before you into singing, and all the
trees of the field shall clap their hands.*
ISAIAH 55:12 KJV

God reveals Himself in a million different ways, but
perhaps the most breathtaking is through nature. The
next time you're in a mountainous spot, pause and
listen. Can you hear the sound of God's eternal song?
Does joy radiate through your being? Aren't you filled
with wonder and with peace? The Lord has, through
the beauty of nature, given us a rare and glorious gift.

---

*When I view the wonders of Your marvelous creation,
Lord, my heart fills with absolute joy! Amen.*

DAY 61
A Valuable Deposit

*He anointed us, set his seal of ownership
on us, and put his Spirit in our hearts as a
deposit, guaranteeing what is to come.*
2 CORINTHIANS 1:21–22 NIV

When we commit our lives to Christ, He doesn't let
us flail around in this mixed-up world without any
help. We have the deposit of the Holy Spirit with us
all the time, and He also gives us His Word and the
help of other Christians to keep us strong in the Lord.
So whenever you feel alone or overwhelmed with life,
remember that God has anointed you, set His seal upon
you, and deposited the Holy Spirit right inside your
heart. That is the most valuable deposit of all!

---

*Dear Lord, thank You for depositing
Your Holy Spirit in my heart to lead and
guide me. Help me to listen. Amen.*

DAY 62
Never Lost for Long

*For "whoever calls on the name of
the Lord shall be saved."*
ROMANS 10:13 NKJV

You call out to God, but maybe for a little while you
don't hear anything. You may have to listen intently for
a while, but eventually you are reassured by His voice.
When He calls your name, you know you are safe. You
may have to take a few steps in the dark, but by moving
toward Him, you eventually see clearly. A light comes
on in your heart, and you recognize where you are and
what you need to do to get back on the path God has
set before you.

---

*Heavenly Father, help me to stay focused on
You. Show me how to remove distractions from
my life so I can stay close to You. Amen.*

DAY 63
Infinite and Personal

Am I a God at hand, saith the LORD, and not a God afar off? . . . Do not I fill heaven and earth?
JEREMIAH 23:23–24 KJV

God says that He is both close at hand and over all there is. Whether your day is crumbling around you or is the best day you have ever had, do you see God in it? If the "sky is falling" or the sun is shining, do you still recognize the one who orders all the planets and all your days? Whether we see Him or not, God tells us He is there. And He's here too—in the good times and bad.

Lord, empower me to trust You when it's hard to remember that You are near. And help me to live thankfully when times are good. Amen.

DAY 64
God-Breathed

*All Scripture is inspired by God and is useful to
teach us what is true and to make us realize what
is wrong in our lives. It corrects us when we are
wrong and teaches us to do what is right.*
2 TIMOTHY 3:16 NLT

God's Word continues to be God-breathed! It is as
relevant today as it ever was! Scripture speaks to us
in our current situations just as it did to people a
few thousand years ago. . .just as it will for eternity.
Situations and cultures and languages and technolo-
gies have changed all throughout history, but God has
been able to speak to people exactly where they are
through His living Word. There is certainly no other
book, collection of books, or any other thing in the
world that can do that. Only the living Word, which
continues to be God-breathed.

*Dear God, all things pass into history except
for You and Your Word. How wonderful it is
that Your Word transcends time, is relevant in
the present, and will live forever! Amen.*

DAY 65
Never Alone

*"But the Advocate, the Holy Spirit, whom the Father
will send in my name, will teach you all things and
will remind you of everything I have said to you."*
JOHN 14:26 NIV

Jesus called the Holy Spirit "the Advocate," a translation
of the Greek word *parakletos*: "one called alongside to
help." It can also indicate "strengthener," "comforter,"
"helper," "adviser," "counselor," "intercessor," "ally," and
"friend." The Holy Spirit walks with us to help, instruct,
comfort, and accomplish God's work on earth. Through
His presence inside us, we know the Father. In our deepest time of need, He is there. He comforts and reveals
to us the truth of God's Word. Jesus is always with us
because His Spirit lives in our hearts. No Christian
ever walks alone!

---

*Strengthener, comforter, helper, adviser, counselor,
intercessor, ally, friend—oh, Holy Spirit of God!
Thank You for dwelling within my heart, guiding
me, and drawing me near to the Father. Amen.*

DAY 66
Mercy Multiplied

Mercy unto you, and peace, and love, be multiplied.
JUDE 1:2 KJV

Have you ever done the math on God's mercy? If so, you've probably figured out that it just keeps multiplying itself out, over and over again. We mess up; He extends mercy. We mess up again; He pours out mercy once again. In the same way, peace, love, and joy are multiplied back to us. Praise the Lord! God's mathematics work in our favor.

Father God, I am so thankful that Your math works differently than mine! Amen.

Everyday Joy

For in him we live, and move, and have our being.
ACTS 17:28 KJV

Every breath we breathe comes from God. Every step we take is a gift from our Creator. We can do nothing apart from Him. In the same sense, every joy, every sorrow—God goes through each one with us. His heart is for us. We can experience joy in our everyday lives, even when things aren't going our way. We simply have to remember that He is in control. We have our being. . .in Him!

Thank You for being in control of all things, God. I would rather have You by my side than anyone else in the world. Through every up, down, and in between, You are there! Amen.

DAY 68
Chosen

"Before I formed you in the womb I knew you
[and approved of you as My chosen instrument],
and before you were born I consecrated you."
JEREMIAH 1:5 AMP

God said that before He formed Jeremiah in his mother's womb, He knew him. God separated him from everyone else to perform a specific task, and He consecrated him for that purpose. We can be sure that if God did that for Jeremiah, He did it for each one of us. Nothing about us or our circumstances surprises God. He knew about everything before we were born. And He ordained that we should walk in those ways because we are uniquely qualified by Him to do so. What an awesome God we serve!

Father, the thought that You chose me before the
foundation of the world and set me apart for a
specific calling is humbling. You are so good. May I
go forward with a renewed purpose in life. Amen.

DAY 69

Truth

*"You will know the truth,
and the truth will set you free."*
JOHN 8:32 NLT

What lies do you believe about yourself? How might those lies be preventing you from experiencing God's plan for your life? The next time you're tempted to believe a lie, write it down. Then find a scripture passage that speaks truth over the situation. Write that scripture verse across the lie. Commit the truth to memory. Over time, God's Word will transform your thinking and you'll begin to believe the truth. Then something amazing will happen: you'll be set free.

---

*Father, thank You for the truth Your Word
speaks about my life. Open my eyes to the
truth and help me to believe it. Amen.*

Hold His Hand

"For I am the LORD your God who takes hold of your right hand and says to you, Do not fear; I will help you."
ISAIAH 41:13 NIV

God desires to help us. When we walk through life hand in hand with God, we can face anything. His love covers us. His presence is our guard. We can do all things through Christ because we are given His strength. Do you feel as though you're walking through life alone? Do not fear. Are you in need of love, protection, courage, and strength? Reach out your hand. Allow Jesus to take hold of it. Receive His love and protection. Bask in His courage and strength. Take hold of His hand!

Dear Lord, thank You that I do not have to fear. You will help me by taking my hand. Amen.

Our Rock and Savior

"The LORD lives! Praise be to my Rock!
Exalted be my God, the Rock, my Savior!"
2 SAMUEL 22:47 NIV

Throughout the Psalms, we read that David not only worshiped and praised God but complained to Him, was honest with God about what he was feeling, and even admitted to being angry at God. Perhaps the most amazing thing about David, though, was his constant devotion and reliance on his Creator. Even though David is the powerful king of Israel, he praises God in 2 Samuel 22:47, calling Him his rock and Savior. David knew that God was alive, and he also knew that he needed Him more than anything else in the world. It's the same for us today!

Dear Lord, You are my rock and my Savior.
You are alive, and I praise You as God above all
else. Thank You for Your love and power. Amen.

God in the Details

*"When we heard of it, our hearts melted in
fear and everyone's courage failed because
of you, for the LORD your God is God in
heaven above and on the earth below."*
JOSHUA 2:11 NIV

Sometimes, when our lives seem to be under siege
from the demands of work, bills, family, whatever—
finding the work of God amid the strife can be difficult. Even though we acknowledge His power, we may
overlook the gentle touches, the small ways in which He
makes every day a little easier. Just as the Lord cares for
the tiniest bird (Matthew 10:29–31), so He seeks to be
a part of every detail in your life. Look for Him there.

*Father God, I know You are by my side every
day, good or bad, and that You love and care for
me. Help me to see Your work in my life and in
the lives of my friends and family. Amen.*

Finishing with Joy

But none of these things move me,
neither count I my life dear unto myself,
so that I might finish my course with joy.
ACTS 20:24 KJV

The Christian life is a journey, isn't it? We move from point A to point B, and then on from there—all the while growing in our faith. Instead of focusing on the ups and downs of the journey, we should be looking ahead to the finish line. We want to be people who finish well. Today, set your sights on that unseen line that lies ahead. What joy will come when you cross it!

Father God, help me to keep my eyes on the finish
line so I can finish my journey with joy. Amen.

Sense of Belonging

"All that the Father gives Me will come to Me, and the one who comes to Me I will by no means cast out."
JOHN 6:37 NKJV

We belong to Christ. When the Father calls us to come to Jesus, we belong to Him. This is an irrevocable transaction. We are His, given to Him by the Father. He does not refuse to save us. He will not refuse to help us. No detail of our lives is unimportant to Him. No matter what happens, He will never let us go. Like the enduring love of a parent—but even more perfect—is the love of Christ for us. He has endured all the temptations and suffered all the pain that we will ever face. He has given His very life for us. We can live peacefully and securely knowing we belong to Him.

Lord Jesus, I confess I often forget that I belong to You and how much You love me. Help me to rest in Your everlasting love and care. Amen.

Seasons of Change

*The Spirit of God, who raised Jesus from the dead,
lives in you. And just as God raised Christ Jesus
from the dead, he will give life to your mortal
bodies by this same Spirit living within you.*
ROMANS 8:11 NLT

Change can be exciting or fearsome. Changing a habit
or moving beyond your comfort zone can leave you
feeling out of control. The power of God that formed
the world, brought the dry land above the waters of the
sea, and raised Jesus from the dead is alive and active
today. Imagine what it takes to overcome the natural
laws of gravity to put the earth and seas in place. Imagine
the power to bring the dead to life again. That same
power is available to work out the details of your life.

---

*Lord, I want to grow and fulfill all You've
destined me to be. Help me to accept change
and depend on Your strength to make the
changes I need in my life today. Amen.*

DAY 76
Joyful Service

Wherefore I put thee in remembrance that thou stir up the gift of God, which is in thee.
2 TIMOTHY 1:6 KJV

This passage is a reminder to every believer. It demonstrates that our God-given gifts remain strong only through active use and fostering. Gifts left unattended or unused become stagnant and, like an unattended fire, die. Just as wood or coal fuels a fire, faith, prayer, and obedience are the fresh fuels of God's grace that keep our fires burning. But this takes action on our part. Are you using the gifts God has given you? Can He entrust you with more? Perhaps today is the day to gather the spiritual tinder necessary to stoke the fire of God within.

God, You have given me special talents and inspiring gifts. I pray, open my eyes to sharing those gifts. Through faith and obedience I will joyfully use them to serve You. Amen.

Practicality vs. Passion

Leaving her water jar, the woman went back to the town and said to the people, "Come, see a man who told me everything I ever did. Could this be the Messiah?"
JOHN 4:28–29 NIV

Practicality gave way to passion the day the woman at the well abandoned her task, laid down her jar, and ran into town. Everything changed the day she met a man at the well and He asked her for a drink of water. Although they had never met before, He told her everything she had ever done, and then He offered her living water that would never run dry. Do you live with such passion, or do you cling to your water jar? Has an encounter with Christ made an impact that cannot be denied in your life?

Lord, help me to lay down anything that stifles my passion for sharing the Good News with others. Amen.

Joyful in Glory

Let the saints be joyful in glory:
let them sing aloud upon their beds.
PSALM 149:5 KJV

When do you like to spend time alone with the Lord?
In the morning, as the stillness of the day sweeps over
you? At night, when you rest your head upon the pillow?
Start your conversation with praise. Let your favorite
worship song or hymn pour forth! Tell Him how blessed
you are to be His child. This private praise time will
strengthen you and will fill your heart with joy!

As I enter into this conversation with You,
Father, I praise You. Thank You for being
Lord—and leader—of my life. Amen.

Sweating the Small Stuff

*Blessed are all who fear the LORD, who walk in
obedience to him. You will eat the fruit of your
labor; blessings and prosperity will be yours.*
PSALM 128:1–2 NIV

The Lord showers us with many blessings each day—
family, friends, education, job, good health, and a beautiful earth. But despite the gifts He gives, it's easy to
get bogged down in the little things that go wrong.
We're all human, and we sometimes focus on all the
negatives rather than the positives in life. Next time
you're feeling that "woe is me" attitude, remember that
you are a child of God. Spend some time counting all
the wonderful blessings that come from the Lord rather
than the headaches from this earth.

---

*Father, thank You that I am Your child.
Remind me each day to count the many blessings
You shower upon me rather than focusing
on the negatives of this world. Amen.*

DAY 80
Prayer

Jesus often withdrew to lonely places and prayed.
LUKE 5:16 NIV

Jesus is our perfect role model. If He withdrew often to pray, shouldn't we? Do we think we can continually give to others without getting replenished ourselves? Make prayer a priority. Recognize that the Lord must daily fill your cup so that you will have something to give. Set aside a specific time, a specific place. Start slow. Give Him five minutes every day. As you are faithful, your relationship with Him will grow. Over time you will crave the time spent together as He fills your cup to overflowing. Follow Jesus' example and pray!

Dear Lord, help me set aside time to pray each day. Please fill my cup so that I can share with others what You have given me. Amen.

Marvelous Plans

*L<small>ORD</small>, you are my God; I will exalt you and praise
your name, for in perfect faithfulness you have
done wonderful things, things planned long ago.*
I<small>SAIAH</small> 25:1 <small>NIV</small>

God has a "promised land" for us all—a marvelous plan
for our lives. Recount and record His faithfulness in your
life in the past, because God has already demonstrated
His marvelous plans to you in so many ways. Then
prayerfully anticipate the future journey with Him. Keep
a record of God's marvelous plans in a journal as He
unfolds them day by day. You will find God to be faithful
in the smallest aspects of your life and oh-so-worthy of
your trust.

---

*Oh Lord, help me to recount Your faithfulness,
record Your faithfulness, and trust Your faithfulness
in the future. For You are my God, and You have
done marvelous things, planned long ago. Amen.*

DAY 82
Smile, Smile, Smile

*"I will forget my complaint, I will
change my expression, and smile."*
JOB 9:27 NIV

Days may not go just as planned. We are all human, and
we can't always control our circumstances. What we can
control, however, is our attitude. Remember each day that
you are a representative of Jesus Christ. As a Christian
and a woman, it is important to model a godly attitude
at all times. Even a small look or smile can help show
others the love of God. Just because we don't feel like
having a good attitude doesn't mean we shouldn't try.
God tells us to praise Him always—in good times and
in bad. Let that praise show on your face today.

---

*Lord, I know I can choose my attitude. Help me to
show Your love to others by having a positive attitude
each day. Let Your glory show on my face. Amen.*

Your Glorious Future

*"No eye has seen, no ear has heard,
and no mind has imagined what God has
prepared for those who love him."*
1 CORINTHIANS 2:9 NLT

God's promise for our future is so magnificent that we can't even comprehend it. He has great plans for each of us, but we often become paralyzed by fear. Why? Because the past seems more comfortable. Because the future is uncertain. While God doesn't give us a map of what our future is like, He does promise that it will be more than we could ever ask or imagine. What steps of faith do you need to take today to accept God's glorious future for your life?

*God, Your ways are not my ways and Your plans
are too wonderful for me to even comprehend.
Help me to never be satisfied with less than
Your glorious plans for my life. Amen.*

DAY 84
He Hears Me

I love the LORD because he hears my
voice and my prayer for mercy.
PSALM 116:1 NLT

Isn't that mind-blowing? The almighty God of the universe who created and assembled every particle in existence hears us when we come before Him. Maybe we go to the Lord in song, praising. Maybe we spend some time reading and thinking about God's Word. Maybe we are praying to Him as we reach out for His comfort. Whatever we do, God hears us and is interested in what we have to say. Isn't that a great reason to love the Lord? May we never forget to give thanks to God daily for the opportunity that He provides us simply to be heard.

I have so many reasons to love You, Lord, so many reasons to worship and praise You. How grateful I am that You hear my voice! I love You, Lord. Amen.

Life Preservers

My comfort in my suffering is this:
Your promise preserves my life.
PSALM 119:50 NIV

In the difficulties of life, God is our life preserver. When we are battered by the waves of trouble, we can expect God to understand and to comfort us in our distress. His Word, like a buoyant life preserver, holds us up in the bad times. But the life preserver only works if you put it on *before* your boat sinks. God will surround you with His love and protection—even if you're unconscious of His presence. He promises to keep our heads above water in the storms of life.

Preserving God, I cling to You as my life preserver.
Keep my head above the turbulent waters so I don't
drown. Bring me safely to the shore. Amen.

A Sacrifice of Praise

Is any among you afflicted? let him pray.
Is any merry? let him sing psalms.
JAMES 5:13 KJV

It's tough to praise when you're not feeling well, isn't it? But that's exactly what God calls us to do. If you're struggling today, reach way down deep. Out of your pain, your weakness, offer God a sacrifice of praise. Spend serious time in prayer. Lift up a song of joy—even if it's a weak song! You'll be surprised how He energizes you with His great joy!

I'm struggling today, God. But that's no surprise to You, is it? You know just how I feel. Please energize my sluggish spirit. I want to sing praises to You! Amen.

Our Confidence

*Do not be afraid of sudden terror, nor of trouble from
the wicked when it comes, for the LORD will be your
confidence, and will keep your foot from being caught.*
PROVERBS 3:25–26 NLT

Whether our loved ones are in harm's way daily or
not, all of us live in a dangerous world. And while we
should take physical precautions, our best preparation
is spiritual. When we spend time with God and learn
about His love for us and our families, we begin to
realize that He will give us His grace when we need it.
He promises to never leave us; and the more we come
to know His love, the more we will rest in that promise.

---

*God, thank You that You promise Your peace
to those who seek You. Help me to rest in
Your love for my family and me. Amen.*

DAY 88
Redemption

Put your hope in the LORD, for with the LORD is
unfailing love and with him is full redemption.
PSALM 130:7 NIV

When God permits a redemption, or "buying back," of lost years and relationships, we get a black-and-white snapshot of the colorful mural of God's redemption of us in Christ. When we one day stand in His presence, we'll understand more clearly the marvelous scope of God's redeeming love in ways we cannot now begin to imagine—in broken relationships we thought could never be restored.

I praise You, Father, for Your awesome redemption.
Thank You that I've yet to see the scope of it all. Amen.

A Shadow of the Past

"Only Rahab the prostitute and all who are with her in her house shall be spared, because she hid the spies we sent."

JOSHUA 6:17 NIV

Rahab wasn't trapped by her past. It didn't hold her back. She was used by God. Her name has come down to us centuries later because of her bold faith. We all have to deal with a past, but God is able to bring good from a painful past. By the grace and power of God, we can make choices in the present that can affect our future. There is transforming power with God. We have hope, no matter what lies behind us.

Holy Spirit, You are always at work. Don't ever stop! Show me a new way, Lord. Help me to make healthier choices for myself and my family. Thank You for Your renewing presence in my life. Amen.

Pour Out Prayers

*Trust in Him at all times, you people; pour out
your heart before Him; God is a refuge for us.*
PSALM 62:8 NKJV

The psalmist tells us to trust the Lord at all times and to
pour out our hearts to Him. There is nothing we think
or feel that He does not already know. He longs for us
to come to Him, spilling out our thoughts, needs, and
desires. God invites us to an open-ended conversation.
He made us for relationship with Him. He never tires
of listening to His children. The Lord is our helper. He
is our refuge. He knows the solutions to our problems
and the wisdom we need for living each day.

---

*Lord, remind me of Your invitation to
pour out my problems to You. You are my
refuge and my helper. Help me to trust You
with every detail of my life. Amen.*

Three in One

*I am Alpha and Omega, the beginning
and the end, the first and the last.*
REVELATION 22:13 KJV

What makes our God unique among the religions of
the world? No other religion has a God whose Son is
equal to the Father. The Jews and Muslims reject the
idea of God having a Son. Only Christianity has a
triune God—three persons in one God. The Bible is
unique because in it God fully reveals who He is. Since
Jesus is fully God, let it renew our hope and faith in
our Savior. He who created all things out of nothing
will re-create this world into a paradise without sin.

---

*Jesus, I learn how to live by Your human example,
and I trust in You as my God—Father, Son, and Holy
Spirit—three persons, one God, one perfect You! Amen.*

Charm Bracelet

*But the fruit of the Spirit is love, joy, peace,
patience, kindness, goodness, faithfulness, gentleness,
self-control; against such things there is no law.*
GALATIANS 5:22–23 NASB

A charm bracelet is a beautiful way to commemorate
milestones or special events. Consider your spiritual
charm bracelet. If you had a charm to represent your
growth in each of the traits from Galatians 5, how
many would you feel comfortable attaching to your
bracelet in representation of that achievement? Ask
your Father which areas in your Christian walk need
the most growth. Do you need to develop those traits
more before you feel comfortable donning your bracelet?

---

*Lord, please show me which milestones of
Christian living I need to focus on in order
to have the full markings of the Holy Spirit
in my life. Please help me to grow into the
Christian woman You call me to be. Amen.*

Lasting Treasure

"Beware! Guard against every kind of greed.
Life is not measured by how much you own."
Luke 12:15 NLT

The Lord never meant for us to be satisfied with temporary treasures. Earthly possessions leave us empty because our hearts are fickle. Once we gain possession of one thing, our hearts yearn for something else. Lasting treasure can only be found in Jesus Christ. He brings contentment so that the treasure chests of our souls overflow in abundance. Hope is placed in the Lord rather than our net-worth statement. Joy is received by walking with the Lord, not by chasing some fleeting fancy. Love is showered upon us as we grab hold of real life—life that cannot be bought but that can only be given through Jesus Christ.

Dear Lord, may I be content with what You have
given me. May I not wish for more material
treasures but seek eternal wealth from You. Amen.

I Lift My Eyes

*I lift up my eyes to the mountains—where does
my help come from? My help comes from the
LORD, the Maker of heaven and earth.*

PSALM 121:1–2 NIV

Adulthood is a time when decisions can be the most crucial. Challenges, failures, doubts, and fears may cloud decisions and cripple us into inaction because the end result is unknown. Career paths, relationships, and financial decisions are only some of the areas that cause concern. In all of those things, and in all of life, we shouldn't keep our eyes fixed on the end result, and we shouldn't keep our heads down and simply plow through. Instead, we must lift our eyes to the Lord. If we fix our focus on Jesus, we will see that He is prepared to lead and guide us through all of life's challenges.

Lord, I lift up my eyes to You. Please help me and guide me down the path of life. Let me never become so focused on my own goals or so busy about my work that I forget to look to You, for You are my help. Amen.

Endless Supply of Love

We love because he first loved us.
1 JOHN 4:19 NIV

The power of God's love within us fuels our love when human love is running on empty. He plants His love within our hearts so we can share Him with others. We draw from His endless supply. Love starts with God. God continues to provide His love to nourish us. God surrounds us with His love. We live in hope and draw from His strength, all because He first loved us.

Oh God, the human love I know on earth cannot compare with Your love. When I feel empty, Your love fills me up. Your love is perfect. It never fails. Amen.

DAY 96
Board God's Boat

Then, because so many people were coming and
going that they did not even have a chance
to eat, he said to them, "Come with me by
yourselves to a quiet place and get some rest."
MARK 6:31 NIV

The apostles ministered tirelessly—so much so that
they had little time to eat. The Lord noticed that they
had neglected to take time for themselves. Sensitive to
their needs, the Savior instructed them to retreat by boat
with Him to a solitary place of rest where He was able
to minister to them. Often, we allow the hectic pace of
daily life to drain us physically and spiritually, and in
the process, we deny ourselves time alone to pray and
read God's Word. Meanwhile, God patiently waits. So
perhaps it's time to board God's boat to a quieter place!

Heavenly Father, in my hectic life I've neglected
time apart with You. Help me to board Your
boat and stay afloat through spending time
in Your Word and in prayer. Amen.

Who Exalts?

*No one from the east or the west or from the
desert can exalt themselves. It is God who judges:
He brings one down, he exalts another.*
PSALM 75:6–7 NIV

Sometimes we grumble when others are exalted. We
feel left out. Why do others prosper when everything
around us seems to be falling apart? We can't celebrate
their victories. We aren't joyful for them. Shame on
us! God chooses whom to exalt. . .and when. We can't
pretend to know His thoughts but we *can* submit to His
will and celebrate with those who are walking through
seasons of great favor.

---

*God, it's so hard to be happy for others when I
feel like I haven't been blessed in the same way.
Please help me to rejoice when others experience Your
favor, while I continue to trust that You have a plan
for my life—and that Your plan is good! Amen.*

Always Thinking of You

What is man that You are mindful of him,
and the son of man that You visit him?
PSALM 8:4 NKJV

Have you ever wondered what God thinks about? *You* are always on His mind. In all you think and do, He considers you and makes intercession for you. He knows the thoughts and intents of your heart. He understands you like no one else can. He knows your strengths and weaknesses, your darkest fears and highest hopes. He's constantly aware of your feelings and how you interact with or without Him each day. God is always with you, waiting for you to remember Him and to call on Him for help, for friendship—for anything you need.

Lord, help me to remember You as I go throughout my day. I want to include You in my life and always be thinking of You too. Amen.

DAY 99
His Healing Abundance

Behold, I will bring it health and healing;
I will heal them and reveal to them the
abundance of peace and truth.
JEREMIAH 33:6 NKJV

If we confess our sins to God, He will bring relief to our souls. When we're distressed, we have Jesus, the Prince of Peace, to give us peace. When our emotions threaten to overwhelm us, we can implore Jehovah-Rapha—the God who heals—to calm our anxious hearts. When we're physically sick, we can cry out to Jesus, our great physician. Whether our problems affect us physically, spiritually, mentally, or emotionally, we can trust that God will come to us and bring us healing. And beyond our temporal lives, we can look forward with hope to our heavenly lives. There, we will be healthy, whole, and alive—forever.

Jehovah-Rapha, thank You for healing me.
Help me do my part to seek health and the abundance
of peace and truth You provide. Amen.

DAY 100
Never Settle

*For in him dwelleth all the fulness of the
Godhead bodily. And ye are complete in him.*
COLOSSIANS 2:9–10 KJV

Paul stated clearly that the fullness of deity lives in
bodily form in Christ. He is God the Son, and when
you have God in your heart, you are complete. You
don't need anything added—whether ceremonies or
so-called secret knowledge—to make you *more* complete. If the Spirit of Jesus Christ dwells in your heart
and you are connected to God, you've got it all! Don't
let anyone persuade you otherwise (Colossians 2:8).
Don't settle for substitutes.

*Jesus, You complete me. Since You dwell in
my heart, I am forever connected with God
and heaven. I have all that I need: salvation
and Your perfect, eternal love. Amen.*

A Child in Need

*"For all those things My hand has made,
and all those things exist," says the* LORD. *"But on
this one will I look: on him who is poor and of a
contrite spirit, and who trembles at My word."*
ISAIAH 66:2 NKJV

A humble child of God with a need catches His eye.
Though He is always watching over all of us, He is
drawn to a child who needs Him. We may need forgiveness, wisdom, courage, endurance, patience, health,
protection, or even love. God promises to come to our
aid when He sees us with a hand up, reaching for His
assistance. What needs do you have in your life today?
Raise your hand in prayer to God. He'll take care of
your needs and then some—blessing your life in ways
you can't even imagine!

---

*Father, thank You for caring about the needs
of Your children. Help me to remember
to always seek You first. Amen.*

Pressed Down, Running Over

*Give, and it shall be given unto you; good
measure, pressed down, and shaken together, and
running over, shall men give into your bosom.*
LUKE 6:38 KJV

"Give, and it shall be given unto you." Likely, if you've
been walking with the Lord for any length of time,
you've heard this dozens of times. Do we give so that
we can get? No, we give out of a grateful heart, and
the Lord—in His generosity—meets our needs. Today,
pause and thank Him for the many gifts He has given
you. Do you feel the joy running over?

---

*Lord, help me to always give from a grateful heart
and never because I plan to get something in return.
You have given me abundant blessings, Father.
Thank You for always meeting my needs. Amen.*

DAY 103
The Perfect Reflection

"Give careful thought to your ways."
HAGGAI 1:7 NIV

As we give careful thought to our ways, we should first look back to where we have come from and reflect on God's work in our lives. We are on a journey. Sometimes the road is difficult; sometimes the road is easy. We must consider where we were when God found us and where we are now through His grace. Even more importantly, we must think about the ways our present actions, habits, and attitude toward God reflect our lives as Christians. Only when we are able to honestly assess our lives in Christ can we call on His name to help perfect our reflection.

Dear Lord, help me to look honestly at the ways I live and make changes where necessary. Amen.

Extend Hospitality

*Do not forget to show hospitality to strangers,
for by so doing some people have shown
hospitality to angels without knowing it.*
HEBREWS 13:2 NIV

The author of Hebrews 13:2, most likely Paul, reminded Christians to extend hospitality to strangers. He suggested that some strangers might even be angels sent from God. Today, most strangers to whom we extend generosity and hospitality are probably not angels, but we can't know if someday God will allow us to entertain an angel without us knowing it. When you practice hospitality, God might be using you to minister to others. What are some ways that you can extend hospitality to strangers?

---

*Lord, teach me to be wise when extending
hospitality to strangers. Enlighten me.
Teach me new ways to minister to others and
show them Your amazing love. Amen.*

The Secret of Serendipity

A happy heart makes the face cheerful.
PROVERBS 15:13 NIV

Can you remember the last time you laughed in wild abandon? Better yet, when was the last time you did something fun, outrageous, or out of the ordinary? Perhaps it is an activity you haven't done since you were a child, like slip down a waterslide, strap on a pair of ice skates, or pitch a tent and camp overnight. A happy heart turns life's situations into opportunities for fun. When we seek innocent pleasures, we glean the benefits of a happy heart. So try a bit of whimsy just for fun, and rediscover the secret of serendipity.

Dear Lord, because of You, I have a happy heart. Lead me to do something fun and spontaneous today! Amen.

Abiding Peace

He himself is our peace.
Ephesians 2:14 NIV

Regardless of life's circumstances, hope and peace are available if Jesus is there. You do not have to succumb to getting buffeted and beaten by the storms of life. Seek refuge in the center of the storm. Run to the arms of Jesus, the Prince of Peace. Let Him wipe your tears and calm your fears. Like the eye of the hurricane, His presence brings peace and calmness. Move yourself closer. Desire to be in His presence. For He Himself is your peace. As you abide in His presence, peace will envelop you. The raging around you may not subside, but the churning of your heart will. You will find rest for your soul.

---

*Dear Lord, thank You for being our peace in
the midst of life's fiercest storms. Amen.*

Confidence

*For I know that my redeemer liveth, and that
he shall stand at the latter day upon the earth:
and though after my skin worms destroy this
body, yet in my flesh shall I see God.*
JOB 19:25–26 KJV

Although we experience various difficulties throughout life, we can still look forward to the blessed future we have. No matter what our struggles are, our Lord is in control. Job had no idea what the purpose of his trial was, but he faced his troubles with confidence, knowing that ultimately he would emerge victorious. Too many times, we view our own situations with self-pity rather than considering God's strength and trusting that His plan is perfect. What peace God offers when we finally cast our cares on Him and with great conviction declare, "I know that my redeemer liveth!"

*O great Redeemer, in You I have confidence,
even when I don't understand life's trials.
Please help me to live victoriously. Amen.*

DAY 108
Never Forgotten

"See, I have engraved you on the palms of my hands."
ISAIAH 49:16 NIV

In the middle of tumultuous times, it's tempting to proclaim that God has forgotten us. Both Israel and Judah struggled with the idea that God had abandoned them. But God took steps to contradict this notion. In an image that prefigures Jesus' crucifixion, God boldly proclaimed that His children were engraved on the palms of His hands. The nail-scarred hands that His Son would endure bear the engraved names of all of us who call upon Him as Savior and Lord. God does not forget us in the midst of our troubles! It is His nail-scarred hand that reaches down and holds our own.

Jesus, the scars on Your hands are because of me—a testament to my salvation.
My name is engraved on Your hand as a child of God. Oh, thank You, dear Jesus! Amen.

A Very Important Phrase

And it came to pass...
FOUND MORE THAN 400 TIMES IN
THE KING JAMES BIBLE

There are times in life when we think we can't bear one more day, one more hour, one more minute. But no matter how bad things seem at the time, they are temporary. What's really important is how we handle the opportunities before us today, whether we let our trials defeat us or look for the hand of God in everything. Every day, week, and year are made up of things that "come to pass"—so even if we fail, we needn't be disheartened. Other opportunities—better days—will come. Let's look past those hard things today and glorify the name of the Lord.

Lord Jesus, how awesome it is that You send or allow these little things that will pass. May we recognize Your hand in them today and praise You for them. Amen.

DAY 110
Joyous Freedom

*Blessed is he whose transgression is
forgiven, whose sin is covered.*
PSALM 32:1 KJV

What if you were locked up in a prison cell for years
on end? You waited for the day when the jailer would
turn that key in the lock—releasing you once and for
all. In a sense, experiencing God's forgiveness is like
being set free from prison. Can you fathom the joy?
Walking into the sunshine for the first time in years?
Oh, praise Him for His forgiveness today!

---

*Sweet freedom, Lord. . . It's a beautiful feeling to
have experienced the joy of Your complete and utter
forgiveness. Thank You for setting my spirit free! Amen.*

DAY 111
Focus Time

*In the morning, LORD, you hear my
voice; in the morning I lay my requests
before you and wait expectantly.*
PSALM 5:3 NIV

What is the first thing you do each morning? Many of
us hit the ground running, armed with to-do lists a mile
long. While it doesn't ensure perfection, setting aside a
short time each morning to focus on the Father and the
day ahead can help prepare us to live more intentionally.
During this time, we—like Jesus—gain clarity so that
we can invest our lives in the things that truly matter.

---

*Father, help me to take time each morning to focus on
You and the day ahead. Align my priorities so that the
things I do will be the things You want me to do. Amen.*

The Breath of God

Every part of Scripture is God-breathed
and useful one way or another—showing us
truth, exposing our rebellion, correcting our
mistakes, training us to live God's way.
2 TIMOTHY 3:16 MSG

Do you spend time in God's Word each day? Do you let the breath of God wash over you and comfort you? Are you allowing His Word to penetrate your heart and show you where you've been wrong? If not, you are missing out on one of the most important ways that God chooses to communicate with us today. Ask the Lord for the desire to spend more time in His Word. Don't feel you have the time? Consider listening to an audio version of God's Word as you drive to work or school.

Father, Your Word is so important to me.
Please give me the desire to spend more
time in the Bible each day. Amen.

DAY 113
God Knows

Your eyes saw my unformed body; all the days ordained for me were written in your book before one of them came to be.

PSALM 139:16 NIV

God knows the days of all people. Job said, "A person's days are determined; you have decreed the number of his months" (Job 14:5 NIV). The same knowledge applies to our new birth. He created us anew in Christ Jesus for "good works, which God prepared in advance for us to do" (Ephesians 2:10 NIV). The God who knows everything about us still loves us. With the psalmist, let us declare, "Such knowledge is too wonderful for me, too lofty for me to attain" (Psalm 139:6 NIV).

God, how can You know all about everyone who has lived or ever will live? Your ways are so far beyond my understanding, and yet You love me. You are so wonderful! Amen.

The White Knight

Then I will rejoice in the LORD.
I will be glad because he rescues me.
PSALM 35:9 NLT

We're all waiting for someone to rescue us. We wait and wait and wait. . . The truth is, God doesn't want you to exist in a perpetual state of waiting. Live your life—your whole life—by seeking daily joy in the Savior of your soul, Jesus Christ. And here's the best news of all: He's already done the rescuing by dying on the cross for our sins! He's the *true* white knight who secured your eternity in heaven. Stop waiting; seek His face today!

Jesus, I praise You because You are the rescuer of my soul. Remind me of this fact when I'm looking for relief in other people and places. You take care of my present and eternal needs, and for that I am grateful. Amen.

DAY 115
Eternal Joy!

*And the ransomed of the LORD shall return,
and come to Zion with songs and everlasting
joy upon their heads: they shall obtain joy and
gladness, and sorrow and sighing shall flee away.*
ISAIAH 35:10 KJV

Have you ever pondered eternity? Forever and ever and ever. . . ? Our finite minds can't grasp the concept, and yet one thing we understand from scripture: we will enter eternity in a state of everlasting joy and gladness. No more tears! No more sorrow! An eternal joy fest awaits us! Now that's something to celebrate!

---

*When life becomes difficult, help me to keep things
in perspective, Father. The hardships I face in
the day to day are but blips in time compared
to the eternal joy I will experience in heaven.
Thank You for joy that lasts forever. Amen.*

Praying with Confidence

For we do not have a high priest who is unable to empathize with our weaknesses, but we have one who has been tempted in every way, just as we are— yet he did not sin. Let us then approach God's throne of grace with confidence, so that we may receive mercy and find grace to help us in our time of need.
HEBREWS 4:15–16 NIV

There is no one like a sister. A sister is someone who "gets you." But even a sister's love cannot compare to Christ's love. However you're struggling, help is available through Jesus. Our Savior walked on this earth for thirty-three years. He was fully God *and* fully man. He got dirt under His fingernails. He felt hunger. He knew weakness. He was tempted. He felt tired. He "gets it." Go boldly before the throne of grace as a daughter of God. Pray in Jesus' name for an outpouring of His grace and mercy in your life.

Father, I ask You boldly in the name of Christ to help me. My hope is in You alone. Amen.

He Has Chosen You

*Therefore, as God's chosen people, holy and
dearly loved, clothe yourselves with compassion,
kindness, humility, gentleness and patience.*

COLOSSIANS 3:12 NIV

No matter how athletic, beautiful, popular, or smart you
are, you've probably experienced a time when you were
chosen last or overlooked entirely. Being left out is a
big disappointment of life on earth. The good news is
that this disappointment isn't part of God's kingdom.
Even when others forget about us, God doesn't. He
has handpicked His beloved children now and forever.
The truth is that Jesus died for *everyone*—every man,
woman, and child who has ever lived and will ever live.
The Father chooses us all. All we have to do is grab a
glove and join the team.

*Father, thanks for choosing me. I don't deserve it,
but You call me Your beloved child. Help me to
remember others who may feel overlooked or unloved.
Let Your love for them shine through me. Amen.*

Is Anyone Listening?

"And I will ask the Father, and He will give you another Helper (Comforter, Advocate, Intercessor—Counselor, Strengthener, Standby), to be with you forever."
JOHN 14:16 AMP

Our heavenly Father wants to hear from us. He cares so much that He sent the Holy Spirit to be our Counselor, our Comforter. When we pray—when we tell God our needs and give Him praise—He listens. Then He directs the Spirit within us to speak to our hearts and give us reassurance. Our world is filled with noise and distractions. Look for a place where you can be undisturbed for a few minutes. Take a deep breath, lift your prayers, and listen. God will speak—and your heart will hear.

Dear Lord, I thank You for Your care. Help me to recognize Your voice and to listen well. Amen.

DAY 119

Joy in the Battle

*Then they returned, every man of Judah and
Jerusalem, and Jehoshaphat in the forefront of them,
to go again to Jerusalem with joy; for the LORD
had made them to rejoice over their enemies.*

2 CHRONICLES 20:27 KJV

Enemy forces were just around the bend. Jehoshaphat,
king of Judah, called his people together. After much
prayer, he sent the worshipers (the Levites) to the front
lines, instructing them to sing joyful praises as they
went. The battle was won! When you face your next
battle, praise your way through it! Strength and joy will
rise up within you! Prepare for victory!

---

*No matter what kind of hardship I face, Father God,
I want to praise my way through it and come through
even stronger than I was before. Thank You for helping
me to win life's battles, both large and small. Amen.*

DAY 120
Fences

*"If you keep My commandments, you will abide
in My love, just as I have kept My Father's
commandments and abide in His love."*
JOHN 15:10 NKJV

God's commandments are much like the pasture fence.
Sin is on the other side. His laws exist to keep us in
fellowship with Him and to keep us out of things that
are harmful to us, that can lead to bondage. We abide
in the loving presence of our heavenly Father by staying
within the boundaries He has set up for our own good.
He has promised to care for us and to do the things
needful for us. His love for us is unconditional, even
when we jump the fence into sin. But by staying inside
the boundaries, we enjoy intimacy with Him.

*Father, help me to obey Your commandments
that are given for my good. Thank You
for Your love for me. Amen.*

Christ Is Risen Today!

"He isn't here! He is risen from the dead!"
LUKE 24:6 NLT

The power God used to raise Christ from the dead is the same power we have available to us each day to live according to God's will here on earth. What happened on Easter gives us hope for today and for all eternity. If you haven't accepted Jesus Christ as your personal Savior, take the time right now to start your new life in Christ.

Dear Jesus, thank You for dying on the cross for me and taking away all my sin. You are alive and well, and I praise You today for all You are and all You have done. Amen.

DAY 122

Every Moment

*He will not let your foot slip—he who
watches over you will not slumber.*

PSALM 121:3 NIV

The psalms tell us that God does not sleep. He watches over us, never once averting His eyes even for a few quick moments of rest. God guards our every moment. The Lord stays up all night, looking after us as we sleep. He patiently keeps His eyes on us even when we roam. He constantly comforts us when fear or illness makes us toss and turn. Like a caring parent who tiptoes into a sleeping child's room, God surrounds us even when we don't realize it. We can sleep because God never slumbers.

---

*Oh God, how grateful I am that You never
sleep. When weariness overtakes me,
You guard me like a mother who watches
over her child. I love You, Father! Amen.*

DAY 123
A Comfortable Place

*Don't you realize that your body is the temple of
the Holy Spirit, who lives in you and was given
to you by God? You do not belong to yourself.*
1 CORINTHIANS 6:19 NLT

We take the time to make our homes comfortable and
beautiful when we know visitors are coming. In the
same way, we ought to prepare our hearts for the Holy
Spirit who lives inside of us. We should daily ask God
to help us clean up the junk in our hearts. We should
take special care to tune up our bodies through exer-
cising, eating healthful foods, and dressing attractively
and modestly. Our bodies belong to God. Taking care
of ourselves shows others that we honor God enough
to respect and use wisely what He has given us.

*Dear Lord, thank You for letting me belong to You.
May my body be a comfortable place for You. Amen.*

An Offering of Joy

Then my head will be exalted above the enemies who surround me; at his sacred tent I will sacrifice with shouts of joy; I will sing and make music to the LORD.
PSALM 27:6 NIV

It's one thing to offer a sacrifice of joy when things are going your way and people are treating you fairly. But when you've been through a terrible betrayal, it's often hard to recapture that feeling of joy. As you face hurts and betrayals, remember that God is the lifter of your head. Sing praises and continue to offer a sacrifice of joy!

Lord, lift my head. Wrap me in Your warm embrace. Help me to remember that even though I've experienced betrayal, I can still praise You and offer a sacrifice of joy. I love You, Father! Amen.

Childlike Faith

Don't let anyone look down on you because you are young, but set an example for the believers in speech, in conduct, in love, in faith and in purity.

1 TIMOTHY 4:12 NIV

Much of the wisdom we gain comes through experiences we try to forget in an effort to get back to a purer, more innocent state. Young believers can be a reminder to the older generation of the joy and enthusiasm a pure faith can generate. And they have another important task; after all, "peer pressure" doesn't always have to be negative. The young are best positioned to bring other young folk to God, and that is work fully deserving of respect.

Dear God, help me to rediscover childlike innocence, the simplicity of faith without doubt. It is in that purest form of belief that I am nearest to You. Amen.

Why Not Me?

God gave Paul the power to perform unusual miracles.
When handkerchiefs or aprons that had merely touched
his skin were placed on sick people, they were healed.
ACTS 19:11–12 NLT

When his fellow missionary, Trophimus, fell sick, Paul was given no miracle to help him. When Timothy complained of frequent stomach problems, Paul had no miracle-working handkerchief for Timothy's misery. Paul himself suffered from an incurable ailment (2 Corinthians 12:7), yet he was willing to leave it with God. We too may be clueless as to why God miraculously heals some and not others. Like Paul, we must trust God when there's no miracle. Can we be as resilient as Job who said, "Though he slay me, yet will I trust in him" (Job 13:15 KJV)? We can—waiting for the day when health problems and bad accidents and death cease forever (Revelation 21:4).

When healing doesn't come, Lord Jesus, give me
grace to trust You more. Still I choose hope. Amen.

Be Still

*Thou wilt keep him in perfect peace, whose mind
is stayed on thee: because he trusteth in thee.*
ISAIAH 26:3 KJV

Longing for His children to know His peace, God sent
prophets such as Isaiah to stir up faith, repentance, and
comfort in the hearts of the "chosen people." God's message is just as applicable today as it was back then. By
keeping our minds fixed on Him, we can have perfect,
abiding peace even in the midst of a crazy world. The
path to peace is not easy, but it is simple: focus on God.
As we meditate on His promises and His faithfulness,
He gets bigger, while our problems get smaller.

---

*God, when I focus on the world, my mind and
heart feel anxious. Help me to keep my mind on
You so that I can have hope and peace. Amen.*

Setting Priorities

Cause me to hear Your lovingkindness in the morning,
for in You do I trust; cause me to know the way in
which I should walk, for I lift up my soul to You.
PSALM 143:8 NKJV

Twenty-four hours. That's what we all get in a day.
Though we often think we don't have time for all we
want to do, our Creator deemed twenty-four-hour days
sufficient. How do we decide what to devote ourselves
to? The wisdom of the psalmist tells us to begin the
day by asking to hear the loving voice of the one who
made us. We can lay our choices, problems, and conflicts
before Him in prayer. He will show us which way to go.
Psalm 118:7 (NIV) says, "The LORD is with me; he is my
helper." Hold up that full plate of your life to Him, and
allow Him to decide what to keep and what to let go.

Lord, make me willing to surrender my choices
and activities to You. Cause me to desire
the things You want me to do. Amen.

Joyous Feasts

*The LORD said to Moses, "Speak to the Israelites
and say to them: 'These are my appointed festivals,
the appointed festivals of the LORD, which you
are to proclaim as sacred assemblies.' "*

LEVITICUS 23:1–2 NIV

During the Festival of Tabernacles, the Israelites camped
out in fragile shelters for seven days as a remembrance
of God's care and protection following their escape from
Egypt. This joyous feast took place at the end of the
harvest season and included a time of thanksgiving to
God for the year's crops. Like the Israelites, let's use all
our holidays to celebrate God's goodness, reflecting on
the blessings He has given us personally and as a nation.

---

*Father, the secular world has excluded You
from holidays, especially those set to honor
You. As for me, Lord, I will worship You
on holidays and every day. Amen.*

A Joyous Treasure

*"The kingdom of heaven is like treasure hidden in a field.
When a man found it, he hid it again, and then in his
joy went and sold all he had and bought that field."*
MATTHEW 13:44 NIV

Have you ever stumbled across a rare treasure—one so
priceless that you would be willing to trade everything
you own to have it? If you've given your heart to Christ,
if you've accepted His work on Calvary, then you have
already obtained the greatest treasure of all—new life in
Him. Oh, what immeasurable joy comes from knowing
He's placed that treasure in your heart for all eternity!

---

*Father, thank You for the gift of Your Son.
Because of Your loving sacrifice, I can forever
have joy in my heart knowing that I will
spend eternity in heaven with You. Amen.*

DAY 131
One Thing Is Needed

"Martha, Martha," the Lord answered,
"you are worried and upset about many things,
but few things are needed—or indeed only one."
LUKE 10:41–42 NIV

We are each given twenty-four hours in a day. Einstein and Edison were given no more than Joseph and Jeremiah of the Old Testament. Since God has blessed each of us with twenty-four hours, let's seek His direction on how to spend this invaluable commodity wisely— giving more to people than things, spending more time on relationships than the rat race. In Luke, our Lord reminded dear, dogged, drained Martha that only one thing is needed—Him.

Father God, oftentimes I get caught up in the minutia of life. The piled laundry can appear more important than the people around me. Help me to use my time wisely. Open my eyes to see what is truly important. Amen.

Joy. . .Minute by Minute

*Look straight ahead, and fix your
eyes on what lies before you.*
PROVERBS 4:25 NLT

Ever wonder how you can be perfectly happy one minute
and upset the next? If joy is a choice, then it's one you
have to make. . .continually. We are often ruled by our
emotions, which is why it's so important to stay focused,
especially when you're having a tough day. Don't let
frustration steal even sixty seconds from you. Instead,
choose joy!

---

*Dear heavenly Father, please help me to keep
my emotions in check today—and every day.
If I keep my focus on You and Your goodness,
God, I can always choose joy. Amen.*

God Cares for You

"Consider how the wild flowers grow. They do not labor or spin. Yet I tell you, not even Solomon in all his splendor was dressed like one of these. If that is how God clothes the grass of the field, which is here today, and tomorrow is thrown into the fire, how much more will he clothe you—you of little faith!"

LUKE 12:27–28 NIV

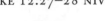

If God makes the flowers, each type unique and beautiful, and sends the rain and sun to meet their needs, will He not care for you as well? He made you. What the Father makes, He loves. And that which He loves, He cares for. We were made in His image. Humans are dearer to God than any of His other creations. Rest in Him. Trust Him. Just as He cares for the birds of the air and the flowers of the meadows, God is in the business of taking care of His sons and daughters. Let Him take care of you.

Father, I am amazed by Your creation.
Remind me that I am Your treasured child.
Take care of me today as only You can do. Amen.

Abide in the Vine

"I am the vine; you are the branches.
If you remain in me and I in you, you will bear
much fruit; apart from me you can do nothing."
JOHN 15:5 NIV

The fruit we bear is consistent with Christ's character. Just as apple trees bear apples, we bear spiritual fruit that reflects Him. Spiritual fruit consists of God's qualities: love, joy, peace, patience, kindness, goodness, faithfulness, gentleness, and self-control. The fruit of the Spirit cannot be grown by our own efforts. We must remain in the vine. How do we abide in Him? We acknowledge that our spiritual sustenance comes from the Lord. We spend time with Him. We seek His will and wisdom. We are obedient and follow where He leads. Abide in the vine and be fruitful!

Dear Lord, help me abide in You so that I may produce fruit as a witness to Your life within me. Amen.

His Love Endures Forever

*God, God, save me! I'm in over my head, quicksand
under me, swamp water over me; I'm going down
for the third time. I'm hoarse from calling for help,
bleary-eyed from searching the sky for God.*
PSALM 69:1–3 MSG

The psalm writers had very real, genuine relationships
with God. They sang praises to God, they got angry with
God, they felt abandoned by God, they didn't under-
stand God's slow response—yet they continued to live
by faith, deeply convinced that God would overcome.
These ancient prayers remind us that nothing can shock
God's ears. We can tell Him anything and everything.
He won't forsake us—His love endures forever.

---

*Oh Lord, You know the secrets of my heart.
Teach me to talk to You through every emotion and
every circumstance. My focus belongs on You. Amen.*

Who Helps the Helper?

*The LORD is my strength and my shield; my heart
trusted in him, and I am helped: therefore my heart
greatly rejoiceth; and with my song will I praise him.*
PSALM 28:7 KJV

Helping can be exhausting. The needs of young children,
teens, grandchildren, aging parents, our neighbors, and
fellow church members—the list is never ending—can
stretch us until we're ready to snap. And then we find
that *we* need help. Who helps the helper? The Lord
does. When we are weak, He is strong. When we are
vulnerable, He is our shield. When we can no longer
trust in our own resources, we can trust in Him. He is
always there, ready to help. Rejoice in Him, praise His
name, and you will find the strength to go on.

---

*Father, I'm worn out. I can't care for all the
people and needs You bring into my life by
myself. I need Your strength. Thank You for
being my helper and my shield. Amen.*

No Matter What

Be thankful in all circumstances, for this is God's will for you who belong to Christ Jesus.
1 THESSALONIANS 5:18 NLT

Jesus enables us to be thankful, and Jesus is the cause of our thankfulness. *No matter what happens,* we know that Jesus has given up His life to save ours. He has sacrificed Himself on the cross so that we may live life to the fullest. And while "to the fullest" means that we will experience pain as well as joy, we must *always* be thankful—regardless of our circumstances—for the love that we experience in Christ Jesus.

Dear Lord, thank You for Your love. Please let me be thankful, even in the midst of hardships. You have blessed me beyond measure. Amen.

DAY 138
My Life

*I long for your salvation, LORD, and your
law gives me delight. Let me live that I may
praise you, and may your laws sustain me.*
PSALM 119:174–175 NIV

Can you really do laundry to please God? Can you
really go to work to please God? Can you really pay the
bills and make dinner to please God? The answer is a
resounding *yes*! Doing all the mundane tasks of everyday
life with gratitude and praise in your heart for all that
He has done for you is living a life of praise. As you
worship God through your day-to-day life, He makes
clear His plans, goals, and dreams for you.

---

*Dear Father, let me live my life to praise You.
Let that be my desire each day. Amen.*

A Strong Spring

My voice shalt thou hear in the morning,
O LORD; in the morning will I direct my
prayer unto thee, and will look up.
PSALM 5:3 KJV

We need to begin our busy days on a strong spring too. Not with just a good cup of coffee but some time spent with our source of strength. Taking five minutes or an hour—or more if we're really disciplined—in prayer and Bible reading can make the difference in our day. No matter if we're facing wresting kids out of bed or fighting traffic all the way to work, that special time can give us a spring in our step today.

Thank You, Lord, for another day. Be my source of strength today. In Jesus' blessed name. Amen.

Magnifying Life

I will boast only in the LORD; let all who are helpless take heart. Come, let us tell of the LORD's greatness; let us exalt his name together.

PSALM 34:2–3 NLT

Mary knew she was the object of God's favor and mercy. That knowledge produced humility. Try as we might, we can't produce this humility in ourselves. It is our natural tendency to be self-promoters. . .to better our own reputations. We need the help of the Spirit to remind us that God has favored each of us with His presence. He did not have to come to us in Christ, but He did. He has chosen to set His love on us. His life redeemed ours, and He sanctifies us. We are recipients of the action of His grace.

Christ Jesus, help me remember what You have done for me and to desire for others to see and know You. Amen.

Thou Shalt Not Worry!

"Do not worry about tomorrow,
for tomorrow will worry about itself.
Each day has enough trouble of its own."
MATTHEW 6:34 NIV

What if the Lord had written an eleventh command-ment: "Thou shalt not worry"? In a sense, He did! He commands us in various scriptures not to fret. So, cast your anxieties on the Lord. Give them up! Let them go! Don't let worries zap your strength and your joy. Today is a gift from the Lord. Don't sacrifice it to fears and frustrations! Let them go. . .and watch God work!

Father God, lift all anxiety from my heart and make my spirit light again. I know that I can't do it on my own. But with You, I can let go. . .and watch You work! I praise You, God! Amen.

All You Need

For your Maker is your husband—the LORD Almighty is his name—the Holy One of Israel is your Redeemer; he is called the God of all the earth.
ISAIAH 54:5 NIV

God is the great "I Am." He is all things that we need. He is our maker. He is our husband. He is the Lord Almighty, the Holy One, the Redeemer, the God of all the earth. He is not a god made of stone or metal. He is not unreachable. He is present. He is near, as close as you will let Him be, and He will meet your needs as no earthly relationship can. Seek the fullness of God in your life. Call upon Him as your Prince of Peace and your King of Glory. He is all that you need—at all times—in all ways.

Oh, Father, be close to me. Fill the empty spots in my heart. Be my husband, my redeemer, and my best friend. Amen.

Renewal of All Things

Peter answered him, "We have left everything to follow you! What then will there be for us?" Jesus said to them, "Truly I tell you, at the renewal of all things, when the Son of Man sits on his glorious throne, you who have followed me will also sit on twelve thrones, judging the twelve tribes of Israel."
MATTHEW 19:27–28 NIV

None of us will just occupy space in heaven. Our God is always productive. And this job to which Jesus refers, that of judging the twelve tribes of Israel, will be given to the disciples. Have you ever speculated as to what you might do in heaven? Well, don't worry; it's not going to be anything like what you've done on earth. Your "boss," after all, will be perfect, and the tasks you perform will be custom-tailored to you. "Job satisfaction" will finally fit into our vernacular.

Lord, I can't even imagine what You have in store for me in heaven. Please keep me faithful to complete the duties You've called me to on earth. Amen.

DAY 144

No More Sting

O death, where is thy sting?
O grave, where is thy victory?
1 CORINTHIANS 15:55 KJV

We have a choice to make. We can either live life in
fear or live life by faith. Fear and faith cannot coexist.
Jesus Christ has conquered our greatest fear—death.
He rose victorious and has given us eternal life through
faith. Knowing this truth enables us to courageously face
our fears. There is no fear that cannot be conquered by
faith. Let's not panic but trust the Lord instead. Let's
live by faith and experience the victory that has been
given to us through Jesus Christ, our Lord.

Lord, You alone know my fears. Help me to
trust You more. May I walk in the victory
that You have purchased for me. Amen.

DAY 145
Look Up!

Your love, LORD, reaches to the heavens,
your faithfulness to the skies.
PSALM 36:5 NIV

In Bible times, people often studied the sky. Looking up at the heavens reminded them of God and His mighty wonders. A rainbow was God's sign to Noah that a flood would never again destroy the earth. God used a myriad of stars to foretell Abraham's abundant family, and a single star heralded Christ's birth. This immense space that we call "sky" is a reflection of God's infinite love and faithfulness. So take time today. Look up at the heavens and thank God for His endless love.

Heavenly Father, remind me to stop and appreciate
Your wonderful creations. And as I look upward,
fill me with Your infinite love. Amen.

What's in Your Heart?

Delight thyself also in the LORD: and he shall
give thee the desires of thine heart.
PSALM 37:4 KJV

Too many times, we look at God's promises as some sort
of magic formula. We fail to realize that His promises
have more to do with our own relationship with Him.
It begins with a heart's desire to live your life in a way
that pleases God. Only then will fulfillment of His
promises take place. The promise in Psalm 37:4 isn't
intended for personal gain—it is meant to glorify God.
God wants to give you the desires of your heart when
they line up with His perfect plan. As you delight in
Him, His desires will become your desires, and you will
be greatly blessed.

Lord, I know You want to give me the
desires of my heart. Help me live in a way
that makes this possible. Amen.

Hold On to Hope

The prospect of the righteous is joy, but the
hopes of the wicked come to nothing.
PROVERBS 10:28 NIV

Trusting in Jesus gave you new life and hope for eternity. So how do you respond when life becomes dark and dull? Does hope slip away? When no obviously great spiritual works are going on, do not assume God has deserted you. Hold on to Him even more firmly and trust. He will keep His promises. Truly, what other option do you have? Without Him, hope disappears.

Dear heavenly Father, the day I met You was the day I received life anew. My soul now overflows with hope, love, peace, and joy. Thank You for saving me! Amen.

Well Watered

*"The LORD will guide you always; he will satisfy your
needs in a sun-scorched land and will strengthen
your frame. You will be like a well-watered
garden, like a spring whose waters never fail."*
ISAIAH 58:11 NIV

We need a downpour of God's Word and the Holy
Spirit's presence in our parched spirits. Not an occasional sprinkle but a soul soaking to replenish our
frazzled bodies and weary minds. We know this soaking
comes from consistent Bible study, the necessary prun-
ing of confessed sin, and prayer time. These produce a
well-watered garden, fruitful and lush, mirroring God's
beauty, creating a life to which others are drawn to come
and linger in His refreshing presence.

*Eternal Father, strengthen my frame,
guide my paths, and satisfy my needs as only
You can. Make my life a well-watered garden,
fruitful for You and Your purposes. Amen.*

DAY 149
Owning Your Faith

But the Helper, the Holy Spirit, whom the Father will send in My name, He will teach you all things, and bring to your remembrance all things that I said to you.

JOHN 14:26 NKJV

Is your faith deeper and stronger than when you first accepted Jesus? While we are responsible for choosing to grow in faith, we can't do it on our own. Jesus promises that the Holy Spirit will teach and guide us if we allow Him to. He will help us remember the spiritual truths we've learned over the years. Fellowship with other Christians also helps us to mature as we share our passions and are encouraged. God wants you to own your faith. Make it real with words and actions.

Jesus, I want to know You intimately. Help me to mature in my walk with You daily. Guide my steps as I seek You through Your Word. Amen.

DAY 150
I Think I Can

"Do not be afraid; only believe."
MARK 5:36 NKJV

Take a trip through the Bible and you'll see that those God asked to do the impossible were ordinary people of their day, yet they demonstrated that they believed God saw something in them that they didn't see. He took ordinary men and women and used them to do extraordinary things. When you believe you can do something, your faith goes to work. You rise to the challenge, which enables you to go further than before, to do more than you thought possible. Consider trying something new—if you think you can, you can!

God, I want to have high expectations. I want to do more than most think I can do. Help me to reach higher and do more as You lead me. Amen.

Everyday Blessings

*But the eyes of the LORD are on those who fear him,
on those whose hope is in his unfailing love.*
PSALM 33:18 NIV

The Lord of all creation is watching our every moment and wants to fill us with His joy. He often interrupts our lives with His blessings: butterflies dancing in sunbeams, dew-touched spiderwebs, cotton-candy clouds, and glorious crimson sunsets. The beauty of His creation reassures us of His unfailing love and fills us with hope. But it is up to us to take the time to notice.

May I always be aware of Your lovely creation, Father God. Your artistry never fails to amaze me! Amen.

A Better Offer

*"So in everything, do to others what
you would have them do to you."*
MATTHEW 7:12 NIV

Jesus took responsibilities, commitments, and obligations seriously. In fact, Jesus said, "All you need to say is simply 'Yes' or 'No'; anything beyond this comes from the evil one" (Matthew 5:37 NIV). Satan desires for us to be stressed out, overcommitted, and not able to do anything well. Satan delights when we treat others in an unkind, offensive manner. However, God, upon request, will help us prioritize our commitments so that our "yes" is "yes" and our "no" is "no." Then in everything we do, we are liberated to do to others as we would have them do to us.

---

*Lord, please prioritize my commitments to
enable me in everything to do to others as I
would desire for them to do to me. Amen.*

Unshakable Love

"For even if the mountains walk away and the hills
fall to pieces, my love won't walk away from you,
my covenant commitment of peace won't fall apart."
The GOD who has compassion on you says so.
ISAIAH 54:10 MSG

We must rest in God's wild, unbending love for us. He promises in Isaiah that no matter what happens, He will never remove Himself from us. When we believe Him wholeheartedly and rest in His love, we will be filled with fear-busting peace and adventurous faith. That faith allows us to dream big dreams and conquer the worries that keep us chained.

Lord, thank You for Your love, which never leaves me.
Help me to rest in Your love above all else. Amen.

Unfailing Love

*I will instruct you and teach you in the way
you should go; I will counsel you with my
loving eye on you. . . . Many are the woes
of the wicked, but the LORD's unfailing love
surrounds the one who trusts in him.*

PSALM 32:8, 10 NIV

God's love surrounds us always—if we trust in Him.
Have you put your complete trust in the Lord? If not,
open your heart to Him and ask Him to become the
Lord of your life. Jesus is standing at the door of your
heart, ready to come in when you respond (Revelation
3:20). Or maybe you've already accepted Christ as your
Savior, but you're not really sure if He can be trusted.
Know that He has been faithful to His children through
all generations and that He is working out every circumstance in your life for your own good (Romans 8:28).

---

*Father God, I praise You for Your unfailing
love. Continue to counsel me and lead me in the
way I should go. Thank You for watching over
me. Help me trust You completely. Amen.*

Equipped to Do God's Will

May the God of peace, who through the blood of the eternal covenant brought back from the dead our Lord Jesus, that great Shepherd of the sheep, equip you with everything good for doing his will, and may he work in us what is pleasing to him, through Jesus Christ, to whom be glory for ever and ever. Amen.

HEBREWS 13:20–21 NIV

Hebrews says God will work in us what is pleasing to Him. When He is at work in you, you may be stretched mentally, emotionally, physically, and spiritually to new places. The good news is that He provides you with everything you need. Like a good football coach wants his team to succeed, God wants His children to receive the blessing of living in His perfect will. You are equipped for the ride!

Father, I ask that You equip me to do Your will in my life. Amen.

An End to Mourning

*"Blessed are those who mourn,
for they will be comforted."*
MATTHEW 5:4 NIV

How often do we think of mourning as a good thing? But when it comes to sin, it is. Those who sorrow over their own sinfulness will turn to God for forgiveness. When He willingly responds to their repentance, mourning ends. Comforted by God's pardon, transformed sinners celebrate—and joyous love for Jesus replaces sorrow.

---

*Heavenly Father, thank You for replacing
my sorrow with joy! Your unconditional love
floods my soul. You are good! Amen.*

Put On a Happy Face

*He restoreth my soul: he leadeth me in the
paths of righteousness for his name's sake.*
PSALM 23:3 KJV

Our God is not a God of negativity but of possibility.
He will guide us through our difficulties and beyond
them. Today, we should turn our thoughts and prayers
toward Him. Focus on a hymn or a praise song and
play it in your mind. Praise chases away the doldrums
and tips our lips up in a smile. With a renewed spirit
of optimism and hope, we can thank the giver of all
things good. Thankfulness to the Father can turn our
plastic smiles into real ones, and as the psalm states,
our souls will be restored.

---

*Father, I'm down in the dumps today.
You are my unending source of strength.
Gather me in Your arms for always. Amen.*

Rejoice!

Rejoice in the Lord always. I will say it again: Rejoice!
PHILIPPIANS 4:4 NIV

When God is the source of our joy, we will never lose that joy. Circumstances may frustrate us and break our hearts, but God is able to supply all our needs. He is able to restore broken relationships. He can give us a new job or help us to succeed at our current job. Through it all, despite it all, we can rejoice in knowing that we are God's and that He loves us.

Dear Father, thank You for loving me.
Help me to make You the source of my joy. Amen.

Get Real

The Lord says: "These people come near to me with their mouth and honor me with their lips, but their hearts are far from me. Their worship of me is based on merely human rules they have been taught."

ISAIAH 29:13 NIV

The world is full of hypocrites. To be honest, sometimes the church is too—hypocrites who profess to know and honor God, but when it comes right down to it, they are only going through the motions of religion. Their hearts are far from Him. Take the time to find out who God is, what He has done for you, and why He is worthy of your devotion. Following God is not about a bunch of man-made rules. He loves you; He sent His Son to die for you; and He longs to have a deep, personal relationship with you. Get real with God and get real with yourself!

Dear God, reveal Yourself to me. Show me who You are and show me how to live so that I honor You not only with my lips, but with my heart as well. Amen.

Trembling While Trusting

*And straightway the father of the child
cried out, and said with tears, Lord,
I believe; help thou mine unbelief.*
MARK 9:24 KJV

When the Lord looks at us, what does He see? Do we
trust Him enough to be vulnerable? Are we willing to
obey even when we are afraid? Do we believe Him?
Do not be afraid to follow Him, and do not let your
trembling hold you back. Be willing to take a step of
faith. If you are scared, God understands and is compassionate and merciful. Fear does not negate His love
for you. Your faith will grow as you trust Him. Let's
trust even while trembling.

*Dear Lord, help my unbelief. Enable me to trust
You even though I may be trembling. Amen.*

Loving Jesus

Looking unto Jesus the author and finisher of our faith.
HEBREWS 12:2 KJV

God is writing a story of faith through your life. What will it describe? Will it be a chronicle of challenges overcome, like the Old Testament story of Joseph? Or a near tragedy turned into joy, like that of the prodigal son? Whatever your account says, if you love Jesus, the end is never in question. Those who love Him finish in heaven, despite their trials on earth. The long, weary path ends in His arms. Today, write a chapter in your faithful narrative of God's love.

God, thank You for helping me write my story.
May my story touch the lives of others and
be a light pointing them to You! Amen.

DAY 162
One Step at a Time

With your help I can advance against a troop; with my God I can scale a wall.
PSALM 18:29 NIV

We often become discouraged when we face a mountain-size task. Whether it's weight loss or a graduate degree or our income taxes, some things just seem impossible. And they often *can't* be done—not all at once. Tasks like these are best faced one step at a time. One pound at a time. Chipping away instead of moving the whole mountain at once. With patience, perseverance, and God's help, your goals may be more attainable than you think.

Dear Father, the task before me seems impossible. However, I know I can do it with Your help. I pray that I will trust You every step of the way. Amen.

Love Your Enemies

"Love your enemies, do good to them, and lend to them without expecting to get anything back. Then your reward will be great."

LUKE 6:35 NIV

God calls us to a love so brave, so intense that it defies logic and turns the world on its side. He calls us to love like He loves. That means we must show patience where others have been short. We must show kindness where others have been cruel. We must look for ways to bless where others have cursed. God promises great rewards for those who do this. Oh, the rewards may not be immediate, but when God promises great rewards, we can know without doubt that any present struggle will be repaid with goodness and blessing, many times over.

Dear Father, help me to love those who hate me, bless those who curse me, and show kindness to those who have been cruel. Help me to love like You love. Amen.

Right People–Right Place–Right Time

*And so find favor and high esteem in
the sight of God and man.*
PROVERBS 3:4 NKJV

God wants you to experience every favor and rich blessing He's prepared. By faith, expect blessing to meet you at every turn. Imagine what your future holds when you become determined to step out to greet it according to God's design. Remain alert and attentive to what God wants to add to your life. Expect the goodness He has planned for you—doors of opportunities are opening for you today!

---

*Lord, thank You for setting favor and blessing
in my path, and help me to expect it wherever
I go and in whatever I do. Amen.*

DAY 165

Turning Bondage into Balance

It is for freedom that Christ has set us free.
Stand firm, then, and do not let yourselves
be burdened again by a yoke of slavery.
GALATIANS 5:1 NIV

The Lord wants us to have a sound mind, which means finding balance in life. How can we be warm, giving, creative, fun, and a light to the world if we are frozen solid in an unmovable block of perfectionism? Let Jesus melt the block of bondage that says, "Never good enough," and let us be able to shout the words, "It is good, and it is finished. Praise God!"

Lord, help me not to be a slave to perfectionism,
but in all things, let me find balance and joy. Amen.

First Love

*But you must continue to believe this truth and stand
firmly in it. Don't drift away from the assurance
you received when you heard the Good News.*
COLOSSIANS 1:23 NLT

Do you remember the day you turned your life over to
Christ? Can you recall the flood of joy and hope that
coursed through your veins? Ah, the wonder of first
love. Like romantic love that deepens and broadens
with passing years, our relationship with Jesus evolves
into a river of faith that endures the test of time.

---

*Father, I am so thankful that You are faithful.
Though human relationships may fail, You are a
constant companion in my life. Thank You! Amen.*

Mirror Image

*Behold, thou art fair, my love; behold,
thou art fair; thou hast doves' eyes.*
SONG OF SOLOMON 1:15 KJV

No matter how hard we try, when the focus is on self, we see shortcomings. Our only hope is to see ourselves through a different mirror. We must remember that as we grow as Christians, we take on the characteristics of Christ. The more we become like Him, the more beautiful we are in our own eyes and to those around us. God loves to behold us when we are covered in Christ. The mirror image He sees has none of the blemishes or imperfections, only the beauty.

---

*Oh God, thank You for beholding me as
being fair and valuable. Help me to see
myself through Your eyes. Amen.*

Thankful, Thankful Heart

I will praise you, LORD, with all my heart;
I will tell of all the marvelous things you have done.
PSALM 9:1 NLT

When you choose to approach life from the positive side, you can find thankfulness in most of life's circumstances. It completely changes your outlook, your attitude, and your countenance. When you are tempted to feel sorry for yourself or to blame others or God for difficulties, push PAUSE. Take a moment and rewind your life. Look back and count the blessings God has given you. Reminding yourself of all He has done for you and in you will bring change to your attitude and give you hope in the situation you're facing. Count your blessings today.

Lord, I am thankful for my life and all You have done for me. When life happens, help me to respond to it in a healthy, positive way. Remind me to look to You and trust You to carry me through life's challenges. Amen.

All the Lonely People

Be devoted to one another in love.
Honor one another above yourselves.
ROMANS 12:10 NIV

As Christians, let's keep an eye out for lonely souls: the people who need a smile and a helping hand, who need a cup of cool water and a listening ear—who need a friend. Let us open our hearts and homes to them. As the book of Romans reminds us, "Be devoted to one another in love. Honor one another above yourselves." This is God's cure for all the lonely people. Amazingly enough, when we reach out to lessen someone else's lonesomeness, perhaps we will ease our own.

Father, give me the desire to live my life for You and for everyone around me. Deepen and enrich my relationships with family and friends. Amen.

What to Do with Free Will

"If you do what is right, will you not be accepted? But if you do not do what is right, sin is crouching at your door; it desires to have you, but you must rule over it."

Every single thing we do every minute of the day involves a choice, and everything has a ripple effect. Everything has consequences. What we eat for breakfast. What books we read, what programs we watch on television, where we go, what we spend our time and money on. Sin is always crouching at our door, but with the help of the Holy Spirit, we can ask it to leave. What will your choices be today?

Holy Spirit, guide me in my decisions. Help me to be wise, clearheaded, and motivated by a selfless love for You and others. Amen.

JOY: Jesus Occupying You

*May all who fear you find in me a cause for
joy, for I have put my hope in your word.*
PSALM 119:74 NLT

Have you ever met someone you immediately knew
was filled with joy? The kind of effervescent joy that
bubbles up and overflows, covering everyone around
her with warmth and love and acceptance. We love to
be near people filled with Jesus-joy. And even more, as
Christians we want to be like them!

---

*Lord, show me how to radiate Your joy in the presence
of others. I want to be a light for You. Amen.*

DAY 172
Stop and Consider

*"Listen to this, Job; stop and consider God's wonders.
Do you know how God controls the clouds and makes
his lightning flash? Do you know how the clouds hang
poised, those wonders of him who has perfect knowledge?"*
JOB 37:14–16 NIV

"Stop and consider My wonders," God told Job. Then
He pointed to ordinary observations of the natural
world surrounding Job—the clouds that hung poised in
the sky, the flashes of lightning. "Not so very ordinary"
was God's lesson. Maybe He was trying to remind us
that there is no such thing as ordinary. Let's open our
eyes and see the wonders around us.

*Oh Father, teach me to stop and consider the
ordinary moments of my life as reminders of
You. Help me not to overlook Your daily care and
provisions that surround my day. Amen.*

When You Give Your Life Away

Which of you, intending to build a tower,
sitteth not down first, and counteth the cost,
whether he have sufficient to finish it?
LUKE 14:28 KJV

Every person has the same amount of life each day. What matters is how you spend it. It's easy to waste your day doing insignificant things, leaving little time for God. The most important things in life are eternal endeavors: Spending time in prayer to God for others. Giving your life to building a relationship with God by reading His Word and growing in faith. Sharing Christ with others and giving them the opportunity to know Him. These are things that will last. What are you spending your life on? What are you getting out of what you give yourself to each day?

Father, please give me wisdom to focus life on the things that matter most. The time I have is precious. Help me to invest it wisely. Amen.

The Trees That Catch the Storm

Brothers and sisters, I could not address you as
people who live by the Spirit but as people who
are still worldly—mere infants in Christ. I gave
you milk, not solid food, for you were not yet
ready for it. Indeed, you are still not ready.

1 CORINTHIANS 3:1–2 NIV

Think of the healthiest trees that shoot up from the
forest floor—they stretch toward the sun and spread
their branches wide. But when the storms of life blow
through, many times it's those towering oaks that will
catch the brunt of the wind. The last thing the enemy
of your soul wants is for you to grow in Christ and His
wisdom. So, expect storms, and be watchful and ready.
But remember too that we can stand strong like the
oak trees. We can know peace in the midst of the gale,
for Christ is the strength in our branches and the light
that gives us life!

Jesus, help me to grow strong in the rich,
nourishing soil of Your love and grace. Amen.

Women Who Loved Well

Charm is deceptive, and beauty is fleeting.
PROVERBS 31:30 NIV

In the end, it will matter to Jesus, of course, that we knew Him as our friend and Savior, but it will also matter that while we walked this earthly life, we loved well. That we saw a need and met it. That we smiled when we wanted to frown. That we were handier with a cup of cool water than with a witty comeback. That we chased after a lost soul faster than we chased after a good time. That we loved other people as ourselves. Those things will matter a great deal, and with the power of the Holy Spirit, all those things are within our grasp. They are also ours to give away—fully, freely, and daily.

Heavenly Father, help me to focus on cultivating those qualities and virtues that are lasting and will make an eternal impact for Your kingdom. Amen.

Forever Joy

We don't look at the troubles we can see now. . . .
For the things we see now will soon be gone,
but the things we cannot see will last forever.
2 CORINTHIANS 4:18 NLT

A painter's first brushstrokes look like random blobs—
no discernible shape, substance, or clue as to what the
completed painting will be. But in time, the skilled
artist brings order to perceived chaos. Initial confusion
is forgotten in joyful admiration of the finished masterpiece. We often can't see past the blobs of trouble
on our life canvases. We must trust that the artist has
a masterpiece underway. And there will be great joy in
its completion.

God, You are the Master Artist. I trust You to
create a masterpiece with my life canvas. Amen.

A New Day

GOD, treat us kindly. You're our only hope.
First thing in the morning, be there for
us! When things go bad, help us out!
ISAIAH 33:2 MSG

Every day is a new day, a new beginning, a new chance to enjoy our lives—because each day is a new day with God. We can focus on the things that matter most: worshiping Him, listening to Him, and being in His presence. No matter what happened the day before, we have a fresh start to enjoy a deeper relationship with Him. A fresh canvas, every twenty-four hours.

Before I get out of bed in the morning, let me say these words and mean them: "This is the day the LORD has made. We will rejoice and be glad in it" (Psalm 118:24 NLT). Amen.

Rejoicing with Friends

*"Then he calls his friends and neighbors together and
says, 'Rejoice with me; I have found my lost sheep.'"*
LUKE 15:6 NIV

Think of all the reasons you have to celebrate. Are you in
good health? Have you overcome a tough obstacle? Are
you handling your finances without much grief? Doing
well at your job? Bonding with friends or family? If so,
then throw yourself a party and invite a friend. Better
yet, call your friends and neighbors together as today's
scripture indicates. Share your praises with people who
will truly appreciate all that the Lord is doing in your
life. Let the party begin!

---

*Lord, thank You that I'm created in the image of a God
who knows how to celebrate. I have so many reasons
to rejoice today. Thank You for Your many blessings.
And today, I especially want to thank You for giving
me friends to share my joys and sorrows. Amen.*

Seek God

*"I love all who love me. Those who
search will surely find me."*
<small>PROVERBS 8:17 NLT</small>

Scripture tells us that God loves those who love Him and that if we search for Him, we will surely find Him. One translation of the Bible says it this way: "Those who seek me early and diligently will find me" (AMP). Seek God in all things and in all ways. Search for Him in each moment of every day you are blessed to walk on this earth. He is found easily in His creation and in His Word. He is with you. Just look for Him. He wants to be found!

Father in heaven, thank You for Your unfailing love for me. Help me to search for You diligently. I know that when I seek, I will find You. Amen.

Even More!

*Now unto him that is able to do exceeding
abundantly above all that we ask or think,
according to the power that worketh in us.*

EPHESIANS 3:20 KJV

"Above all that we ask or think" is just that. Imagine
every good thing that God has promised in His Word—
or things you've only dreamed about. Think of wonderful
things that exceed the limits of human comprehension
or description, then imagine that God is able and *willing*
to do even more! The last part of this verse indicates
that the Holy Spirit works within the Christian's life
to accomplish the seemingly impossible. Our highest
aspirations are within God's power—but like Paul, we
must pray. When we do, God does far more for us than
we could ever guess.

---

*O Lord, You accomplish things I perceive as impossible.
You know my hopes and dreams, and I believe that You
are able to exceed my greatest expectations. Amen.*

Finish Line

*I have fought the good fight, I have
finished the race, I have kept the faith.*
2 TIMOTHY 4:7 NIV

Paul felt that his life was coming to an end. As he
wrote to his friend Timothy, he spoke of this. He was
not boasting; he was just giving his status report, as
it were. Good fight fought? Check. Race finished?
Check (well, almost). Faith kept? Check. What does
your checklist include? What accomplishments make
your list? What goals do you want to be known for
achieving? What do you want to do, who do you want
to become, before your race is finished? Write them
down today. Put a checkbox by each one. Then go and
work out your life, faith, and ministry for all you're
worth. Godspeed.

---

*Dear Lord, bless the work of my hands
and feet. Make me Your servant so that
at the end of my life, I can look forward to
hearing You say, "Well done." Amen.*

Harm for Good

"You intended to harm me, but God intended it for good."
GENESIS 50:20 NIV

Joseph suffered more in his lifetime than any of us ever will. But God remembered him, blessed him, and made him a man of great authority in the land so that he was in the position to make wise decisions and save many people from starvation.

Instead of feeling entitled to apologies, Joseph wanted redemption in place of revenge. In response to his brothers wanting security, he replied, "Don't be afraid. Am I in the place of God? You intended to harm me, but God intended it for good to accomplish what is now being done, the saving of many lives" (verses 19–20).

Maybe you're in the middle of suffering right now, so deep in it you can't possibly see any good. Take encouragement from Joseph's words. You are not God—you cannot see what He sees. Maybe yet there will be some good that comes out of the harm.

Dear God, help me to trust in Your plans. Amen.

DAY 183

Why Me?

I am Alpha and Omega, the beginning and the ending, saith the Lord, which is, and which was, and which is to come, the Almighty.

REVELATION 1:8 KJV

When God spoke our world into existence, He called into being a certain reality, knowing then everything that ever was to happen—and everyone who ever was to be. That you exist now is cause for rejoicing! God made *you* to fellowship with Him! If that fellowship demands trials for a season, rejoice that God thinks you worthy to share in the sufferings of Christ—and, eventually, in His glory. Praise His holy name!

Father, I thank You for giving me this difficult time in my life. Shine through all my trials today. I want You to get the glory. Amen.

Pass It On!

After the usual readings from the books of Moses and the prophets, those in charge of the service sent them this message: "Brothers, if you have any word of encouragement for the people, come and give it."
ACTS 13:15 NLT

Encouragement brings hope. Have you ever received a word from someone that instantly lifted your spirit? Did you receive a bit of good news or something that diminished your negative outlook? Perhaps a particular conversation helped to bring your problems into perspective. Paul passed on encouragement, and many benefited. So the next time you're encouraged, pass it on! You may never know how your words or actions benefited someone else.

Lord, thank You for the wellspring of encouragement through Your holy Word. Amen.

DAY 185
Shine

*"Those who are wise will shine like the brightness
of the heavens, and those who lead many to
righteousness, like the stars for ever and ever."*
DANIEL 12:3 NIV

The next time you are feeling a little frumpy or gray, a little old and tarnished, thank God for the wisdom you have. Think about the best decisions you made in the past year. Then pick yourself up, put on something shiny (an aluminum foil tiara? a bouquet of silverware?), and take your own photo. Print it out and write beneath it, "I shine." Then put it somewhere to serve as a reminder that being wise can be beautiful too.

---

*Dear Lord, thank You for allowing me
to shine with wisdom. Amen.*

Reveal the Hope

In your hearts revere Christ as Lord. Always
be prepared to give an answer to everyone who
asks you to give the reason for the hope that you
have. But do this with gentleness and respect.

1 PETER 3:15 NIV

Isn't the relevance of God's Word amazing? Peter gives three points of advice with several key words. First, set God apart from everything else in your heart; in other words, "sanctify" or recognize God's holiness and treat Him with deserved awe. Second, be prepared to explain your hope in Christ and eternal life, having a full grasp of what and in whom you believe. Finally, remember that *how* you say something is equally important to *what* you say. In other words, we must walk the walk before we can reveal the hope we have in Jesus Christ.

Dear God, please prepare me to explain my hope in
Christ and eternal life. Teach me to explain it in a way
that honors You with gentleness and respect. Amen.

Faith, the Emotion Balancer

That no man is justified by the law in the sight of God, it is evident: for, The just shall live by faith.
GALATIANS 3:11 KJV

Emotions mislead us. One day shines with promise as we bounce out of bed in song, while the next day dims in despair and we'd prefer to hide under the bedcovers. It has been said that faith is the bird that feels the light and sings to greet the dawn while it is still dark. The Bible instructs us to live by faith—not by feelings. Faith assures us that daylight will dawn in our darkest moments, affirming God's presence so that even when we fail to pray and positive feelings fade, our moods surrender to song.

Heavenly Father, I desire for my faith, not my emotions, to dictate my life. I pray for balance in my hide-under-the-covers days so that I might surrender to You in song. Amen.

The Right Focus

Turning your ear to wisdom and applying your heart to understanding—indeed, if you call out for insight and cry aloud for understanding, and if you look for it as for silver and search for it as for hidden treasure, then you will understand the fear of the LORD and find the knowledge of God.

PROVERBS 2:2–5 NIV

Frustration and stress can keep us from clearly seeing the things that God puts before us. Time spent in prayer and meditation on God's Word can often wash away the dirt and grime of the day-to-day and provide a clear picture of God's intentions for our lives. Step outside the pressure and into His presence, and get the right focus for whatever you're facing today.

Lord, help me to avoid distractions and keep my eyes on You. Amen.

Sewing Up
Broken Hearts

He heals the brokenhearted and binds up their wounds.
PSALM 147:3 NIV

A heart that does not feel cannot be broken. But it also cannot love. And a heart that loves deeply can be wounded deeply. But God is the great healer—and He knows how to heal deeply. God searches our hearts and finds the holes. Then He carefully, over time, joins the pieces together—with new love, care, and understanding. A broken heart will never be the same as an innocent one. It is forever scarred. But with the scarring comes wisdom, and that wisdom can blossom into compassion for others who have been hurt as well.

Dear Healer, mend the holes in my heart so I can offer my whole heart to You. Amen.

To Get the Prize

*Everyone who competes in the games
goes into strict training.*
1 CORINTHIANS 9:25 NIV

We are in the race of life. Time is short, but the days are long. We have a lot to do, and we never know when our life will come to an end. All of us are running to the same finish line. It's important that we run our races in a way that shows we are serious about getting the prize—eternal life with Christ. We need to show that we are running toward something worth sacrificing for. And we need to be prepared for whatever falls in our paths—including other runners.

Dear God, please help me "run in such a way as to get the prize" (1 Corinthians 9:24 NIV). Amen.

Strength in Hope

I say to myself, "The LORD is my portion;
therefore I will wait for him."
LAMENTATIONS 3:24 NIV

In this verse, the writer declares that the Lord is his portion. The Lord is our portion too. But when will we fully receive this inheritance and celebrate with Him? We know it is coming, but it's difficult to wait. Hope gives us strength as we anticipate our return to God. We belong to God and know that someday, we will worship Him face-to-face in His presence. Knowing that God will keep His promise, we can say with confidence, "The Lord is my portion; therefore I will wait."

What an amazing promise You have made to me,
Father, that one day I will be with You in heaven!
My hope is in You as I wait for that day. Amen.

DAY 192
Choose Life

"The thief comes only to steal and kill and destroy; I have come that they may have life, and have it to the full."
JOHN 10:10 NIV

God's Word shows us the lie—and the "liar"—behind defeating thoughts. We have an enemy who delights in our believing negative things, an enemy who wants only destruction for our souls. But Jesus came to give us life! We only have to choose it as an act of the will blended with faith. When we rely on Him alone, He'll enable us to not only survive but *thrive* in our daily routine. Each day, let's make a conscious decision to take hold of what Christ offers us—life, to the full.

Loving Lord, help me daily to choose You and the life You want to give me. Give me the eyes of faith to trust that You will enable me to serve lovingly. Amen.

DAY 193
The Word for Every Day

*As for God, his way is perfect; the word of the LORD
is tried: he is a buckler to all them that trust in him.*

2 SAMUEL 22:31 KJV

God's Word is such an incredible gift, one that goes
hand in hand with prayer. It's amazing, really, that
the Creator of the universe gave us the scriptures as
His personal Word to us. When we're faithful to pick
up the Word, He is faithful to use it to encourage us.
Reading and praying through scripture is one of the
keys to finding and keeping our sanity, peace, and joy.

---

*God, thank You for Your gifts of the holy scriptures and
sweet communion with You through prayer. Amen.*

Father God

You are the helper of the fatherless.
PSALM 10:14 NIV

Some of us were blessed with great fathers. These were men who enriched our lives as role models, trainers, encouragers, supporters, huggers, comforters, and friends. But if your father was never there for you or is now gone, run to your Father God and spend some time with Him. Let Him heal the places in you that are hurting and give you the confidence that comes from the only Person in the world who has loved you since before the day you were born—and will continue to love you forever.

Dear Father, hear and bless Your children. Amen.

He Wrote Them Both

God has made the one as well as the other.
ECCLESIASTES 7:14 NIV

We need to learn to see God's grace not just in what He does for us but in what He doesn't do. And we need to realize that the bit of the world we see is just one small piece of a very large story. So when we are standing in the middle of the book and the chapter is a sad and dreary one, we need to remember at least these two things: first, there are many pages to come; and second, it is by God's grace we are living this story, good or bad as it may be.

Dear Author of my life, help me to remember to trust You to write my story. Amen.

An Example Worth Following

I am as a wonder unto many;
but thou art my strong refuge.
PSALM 71:7 KJV

If people follow your example, where will it lead? Will they find themselves headed toward God or away from Him? As you allow God to change you from the inside out, your life will naturally point others in His direction. Being an example worth following doesn't mean you're under pressure to be perfect. It's God's power shining through the lives of imperfect people that whispers most eloquently, "There's more going on here than meets the eye. God is at work."

God, I ask You to take a look in my heart and examine
me. I want You to change me from the inside out
so that my life points others to You. Amen.

Follow the Lord's Footsteps

*Then He said to them, "Follow Me,
and I will make you fishers of men."*
MATTHEW 4:19 NKJV

Jesus asked His disciples to follow Him, and He asks us to do the same. Following Jesus requires staying right on His heels. We need to be close enough to hear His whisper. Stay close to His heart by opening the Bible daily. Allow His Word to speak to your heart and give you direction. Throughout the day, offer up prayers for guidance and wisdom. Keep in step with Him, and His close presence will bless you beyond measure.

---

*Dear Lord, grant me the desire to follow You.
Help me not to run ahead or lag behind. Amen.*

Everlasting Light

*In him was life, and that life was the light of
all mankind. The light shines in the darkness,
and the darkness has not overcome it.*

JOHN 1:4–5 NIV

Focus on the fact that Jesus is the light of the world, who
holds out wonderful hope for us. Set your prayer life to
start with praise and adoration of the King of kings.
Lift your voice in song, or read out loud from the Word.
The Light will eliminate the darkness every time. Keep
your heart and mind set on Him as you walk through
the day. Praise for every little thing; nothing is too small
for God. A grateful heart and constant praise will bring
the Light into your day.

---

*Dear Lord, how we love You! We trust in You this day
to lead us on the right path lit with Your light. Amen.*

DAY 199
Glue

He is before all things, and in him all things hold together.
COLOSSIANS 1:17 NIV

Have you ever felt like your life was falling apart? We need to know that there is someone who is holding us together, even when we feel like falling apart. Jesus has been with us since the beginning. He is "the beginning and the firstborn from among the dead" (verse 18). He can handle our struggles, and He can put us back together again, even if we let everything fall. There is always hope in Him.

Dear Jesus, thank You for being a friend I can always count on. Help me remember to trust You with all the details of my life. Amen.

Know the Hope

*I pray that the eyes of your heart may be
enlightened in order that you may know the
hope to which he has called you, the riches of his
glorious inheritance in his holy people, and his
incomparably great power for us who believe.*

EPHESIANS 1:18–19 NIV

Our heart is central when it comes to God. It's not
only vital for our physical life but for our spiritual life
as well. It's the thinking apparatus of our soul, con-
taining all our thoughts, passions, and desires. Why
was Paul so anxious for Christians to make heartfelt
spiritual progress? Because of the payoff! God freely
offers us His incomparably great power along with a
rich, glorious inheritance. We just have to see our need
for a little surgery.

---

*Instill in me a new heart, God. Fill it with
Your unrivaled power and love. Place within
it the priceless gift of Jesus' sacrifice and the
promise of eternal life in heaven. Amen.*

Annual or Perennial?

They are like trees planted along the riverbank, bearing fruit each season. Their leaves never wither, and they prosper in all they do.
PSALM 1:3 NLT

Annuals or perennials? Each has its advantages. Annuals are inexpensive, provide instant gratification, and keep boredom from setting in. Perennials require an initial investment but, when properly tended, faithfully provide beauty year after year—long after the annuals have dried up and withered away. Perennials are designed for the long haul—not just short-term enjoyment but long-term beauty. The application to our lives is twofold. First, be a perennial—long lasting, enduring, slow growing, steady, and faithful. Second, don't be discouraged by your inevitable dormant seasons. Tend to your soul, and it will reward you with years of lush blossoms.

Father, be the gardener of my soul. Amen.

Why Praise God?

Though he slay me, yet will I trust in him.
JOB 13:15 KJV

It's difficult to praise God when problems press in harder than a crowd exiting a burning building. But that's the time to praise Him the most. We wait for our circumstances to change, while God desires to change us despite them. Praise coupled with prayer in our darkest moments is what moves the mighty hand of God to work in our hearts and lives. How can we pray and praise God when everything goes wrong? The bigger question might be: How can we not?

Jesus, help me to pray and praise You despite my circumstances. Amen.

Morning Orders

*"Have you ever given orders to the morning,
or shown the dawn its place, that it might take the
earth by the edges and shake the wicked out of it?"*

JOB 38:12–13 NIV

God poses many rhetorical questions, all to show the might and wonder and mystery of the Almighty. In these words are some amazing ideas that really cause us to stop and consider who God is. And that is what we should do, especially when we face our worst trials. Stop and consider who God is—that no matter what happens, He will not leave us. . .and that He alone has the answers.

---

*Thank You, God, for providing glimpses
of You in Your Word. Amen.*

DAY 204
Above All

Above all, love each other deeply,
because love covers over a multitude of sins.
1 PETER 4:8 NIV

How deep does your love go? Does it go as far as the distance that grows between two people? Does it cover little insults? Is it deep enough to silence words that should not be said? How deep does your love go? Does it go deep enough to trust? Can it cover over deceit? Does it go deep enough to swallow up betrayal? How deep does Jesus' love go?

Dear Jesus, help me to love as You love. Amen.

God's Delight

Delight thyself also in the LORD: and he shall give thee the desires of thine heart.
PSALM 37:4 KJV

To "delight" in someone is to take great pleasure from simply being in that person's presence. If you truly delight in God, the deepest desire of your heart will be to draw ever closer to Him. This is a desire God Himself delights in filling. That's because God delights in you. You are more than His creation. You are His beloved child. He delights in you like a proud father watching his daughter take her very first steps.

Father please show me the truth of how You see me. I want to believe that You love me unconditionally, but sometimes it's just difficult because of my past. Help me see myself as Your beloved daughter. Amen.

Have You Looked Up?

The heavens proclaim the glory of God. The skies display his craftsmanship. Day after day they continue to speak; night after night they make him known.
PSALM 19:1–2 NLT

God has placed glimpses of creation's majesty—evidence of His love—throughout our world. Sunsets, seashells, flowers, snowflakes, changing seasons, moonlit shadows. Such glories are right in front of us, every single day! But we must develop eyes to see these reminders in our daily life and not let the cares and busyness of our lives keep our heads turned down. Have you looked up today?

Lord, open my eyes! Unstuff my ears!
Teach me to see the wonders of Your creation every
day and to point them out to others. Amen.

Reap in Joy!

*Remember this: Whoever sows sparingly
will also reap sparingly, and whoever sows
generously will also reap generously.*
2 CORINTHIANS 9:6 NIV

Each of us wants to feel appreciated, and we like to deal with a friendly person. Have you ever worked with a person who seemed to have a perpetually bad attitude? You probably didn't feel particularly encouraged after an encounter with this coworker. Yes, sometimes things go wrong, but your attitude in the thick of it is determined by your expectations. If you expect things to turn out well, you'll generally have a positive mental attitude. Treat everyone with genuine kindness, courtesy, and respect, and that is what will be reflected back to you.

Heavenly Father, help me plant the seeds of patience, love, compassion, and courtesy in all those I come in contact with. Please let me make an eternal difference in these people's lives. I want to joyfully reap a rich harvest for Your kingdom. Amen!

Our Great Contender

*You have seen it, Lord, do not keep silent; Lord,
do not be far from me. Stir Yourself, and awake
to my right and to my cause, my God and my
Lord. Judge me, Lord my God, according to Your
righteousness, and do not let them rejoice over me.*
PSALM 35:22–24 NASB

Our Lord God is the greatest warrior of all time. He
is our guide, our leader, our defender, our shield. He
is all-powerful, all-knowing, all-mighty, and all good.
Why would we ever hesitate to call on Him? Why
would we ever think that our own strength could
somehow be diminished by being supported by the
Creator of the universe? The next time you find yourself
facing a battle, don't wait. Don't try to do it on your
own. Don't stand up by yourself. Ask God to contend
for you.

*Almighty God, please defend me from my
enemies and help me fight my battles. Amen.*

Our Song

*By day the L<small>ORD</small> directs his love, at night his song
is with me—a prayer to the God of my life.*
P<small>SALM</small> 42:8 <small>NIV</small>

All through the Bible, we find people worshiping God
through song. They sing to God about winning battles
and the birth of babies. They sing songs of lament and
songs of praise, songs sinking with sorrow and songs
bouncing with joy. There is, of course, a whole book
devoted just to this exercise: Psalms. By day, God guides
us; and at night, He still leaves the doors of communication open. What do you think His song is saying
to you? What do you want to sing to Him?

*Dear God, help me listen for Your song, and help me
find the words to sing praise to You every day. Amen.*

Expect Great Things

*Be of good courage, and he shall strengthen
your heart, all ye that hope in the LORD.*
PSALM 31:24 KJV

Trusting God can help transform you into a "glass half
full" kind of person. You can face every day, even the
tough ones, with confidence and expectation because
you're aware there's more to this life than can be seen.
You can rest in the promise that God is working all
things together for your good. You know death is not
the end. In other words, you can expect that great things
lie ahead. Why not anticipate them with thanks and
praise?

---

*I praise You, Lord, for who You are and Your
great plans for me. I trust You to work out all
things for my good and for Your glory. Amen.*

DAY 211
Faultless

*To him who is able to keep you from stumbling
and to present you before his glorious presence
without fault and with great joy.*
JUDE 1:24 NIV

Jesus loves us so much, despite our shortcomings. He
is the one who can keep us from falling—who can
present us faultless before the Father. Because of this,
we can have our joy restored no matter what. Whether
we have done wrong and denied it or have been falsely
accused, we can come into His presence to be restored
and lifted up. Let us keep our eyes on Him instead of
on our need to justify ourselves to God or others.

---

*Thank You, Jesus, for Your cleansing love and for
the joy we can find in Your presence. Amen.*

Confident Hope

*For you have been my hope, Sovereign
LORD, my confidence since my youth.*
PSALM 71:5 NIV

Internal clues suggest that the psalmist wrote Psalm 71
during a troublesome time. In the midst of recounting
his situation, he asserted that God had been his hope
and confidence since his youth. As Paul later out-
lined in Romans 5, his previous experiences built that
hope. Confidence in the Lord allows us to face disasters
without fear (Proverbs 3:25–26), to live in peace (Isaiah
32:17), and to approach God (Ephesians 3:12). In an
unpredictable world, we serve an unchanging God who
has earned our confidence.

---

*Father, in this ever-changing, fast-paced world, I find
comfort knowing that You never change. My confidence
is in You with a good outcome guaranteed. Amen.*

DAY 213
Planting

I planted the seed, Apollos watered it,
but God has been making it grow.
1 CORINTHIANS 3:6 NIV

Have you ever hesitated to engage in a spiritual discussion with a person because you didn't know how he would take it or you felt like you didn't have the time required to build a relationship with him? Of course, in an ideal world, we'd have time to sit and chat with everyone for days and the coffee would be free. But the fact that our world isn't ideal should not prevent us from planting a seed. You just never know what might happen to it. And that makes for some exciting gardening.

Dear God, thank You for allowing me to work for Your kingdom. Help me to plant more seeds. Amen.

DAY 214
The Answer Is No One

The LORD is my light and my
salvation—whom shall I fear?
PSALM 27:1 NIV

When you accept Christ as your Savior, you get certain things in return. You get an understanding of good and evil—and you get the knowledge that you are on the side of good. You get a clearer vision of the darkness in your life—and you get a friend who is always with you, no matter how dark things seem to be. And you get peace through knowing your place before God, standing in His grace blameless and pure, and anticipating a place in heaven created just for you—a place no one can take away.

Dear Jesus, help me to feel You at my side. Amen.

Hope Thrives

"For I know the plans I have for you,"
declares the LORD, "plans to prosper you and not to
harm you, plans to give you hope and a future."
JEREMIAH 29:11 NIV

Hope thrives in the fertile soil of a heart restored by a loving gesture, a compassionate embrace, or an encouraging word. It is one of God's most precious gifts. God *wants* to forgive our sins and lead us on the paths of righteousness—just as He did for the Israelites of old. He has great plans for us. That's His promise, and our blessed hope.

Father, You provide hope when all seems
hopeless. Trusting in Your plans for me brings
me joy. My future is in Your hands, so how
can it be anything but good? Amen.

Reflecting God
in Our Work

*Whatever you do, work at it with all your heart,
as working for the Lord, not for human masters.*
COLOSSIANS 3:23 NIV

As believers, we are God's children. No one is perfect, and for this there is grace. However, we may be the only reflection of our heavenly Father that some will ever see. Our attitudes and actions on the job speak volumes to those around us. Although it may be tempting to do just enough to get by, we put forth our best effort when we remember we represent God to the world. A Christian's character on the job should be a positive reflection of the Lord.

Father, help me today to represent You well through my work. I want to reflect Your love in all I do. Amen.

I Grow Weary

But those who wait for the LORD [who expect, look for, and hope in Him] will gain new strength and renew their power; they will lift up their wings [and rise up close to God] like eagles [rising toward the sun]; they will run and not become weary, they will walk and not grow tired.

ISAIAH 40:31 AMP

As long as we are warring inside, we will not find rest. We must find out what Jesus wants for our lives and then obey. Feasting on His Word and learning more about Him will give us the direction we need and the ability to trust. It is only when we understand our salvation and surrender that we can come to Him, unencumbered by guilt or fear, and lay our head on His chest. Safe within His embrace, we can rest. We will be as a well-watered garden, refreshed and blessed by our loving Creator.

Father, I am weary and need Your refreshing Spirit to guide me. I trust in You. Amen.

DAY 218
The Worrier's Psalm

Do not fret.
PSALM 37:1 NIV

Instead of fretting, delight in the Lord, and He will give you all your heart's desires—especially if one of those desires is to be free from fretting. And even if you've prayed, breathed, and tried to relax, and the worries still come (like houseflies that just refuse to find their way back out the screen), then don't fret about fretting. Trust. Commit. Be still. Wait. Refrain. Turn. Give generously. Lend freely. Do good. Hope. Consider. Observe. Seek peace. Just don't fret.

Dear God, you know our hearts and the worries that prey on our minds. Please help us to stay busy doing good and to grow in trust and patience. Please help us to let go of control we never had to start with. Amen.

DAY 219
Living the "What If" Blues

And we know that in all things God works
for the good of those who love him, who have
been called according to his purpose.
ROMANS 8:28 NIV

All of life's "not knowing" can prompt a lot of "what ifs." Pray for wisdom and guidance, knowing that God will give them to you freely and lovingly. But if you still take a wrong turn, embrace His promise that He will work all things for good for those who love Him. It's hard to imagine, but the Lord really does mean "all things." Praying and embracing His promises will go a long way toward keeping you on the right road, as well as easing those "what if" blues.

God, I'm so grateful You can turn evil into
good and sorrow into joy. Amen.

Expectant Hope

*In the morning, LORD, you hear my
voice; in the morning I lay my requests
before you and wait expectantly.*
PSALM 5:3 NIV

God fulfills His side of the bargain to hear our prayers.
Then we take off on our merry way, trying to solve our
dilemma without Him. We leave His presence without
lingering with the Lord to listen and to worship Him
in the silence of our hearts. Then later, we return with
more demands and *gimmes*. God knows our human
hearts and understands. He gently waits to hear from
us—and He delights when we keep our end of the
bargain and linger in His light with hearts full of anticipation and hope.

---

*Dear God, my hope is in You. Thank You for
listening to my prayers and knowing exactly
what I need. I wait patiently, expectantly,
knowing that You will answer me. Amen.*

Just Half a Cup

"I am coming to you now, but I say these things
while I am still in the world, so that they may
have the full measure of my joy within them."
JOHN 17:13 NIV

Our heavenly Father longs to bestow His richest blessings and wisdom on us. He loves us, so He desires to fill
our cup to overflowing with the things that He knows
will bring us pleasure and growth. Do you tell Him to
stop pouring when your cup is only half full? You may
not even realize it, but perhaps your actions dictate that
your cup remain half empty. Seek a full cup, and enjoy
the full measure of the joy of the Lord.

Dear Jesus, forgive me for not accepting the
fullness of Your blessings and Your joy. Help me
to see the ways that I prevent my cup from being
filled to overflowing. Thank You for wanting
me to have the fullness of Your joy. Amen.

The Ultimate Act of Love

Bring joy to your servant, Lord, for I put my trust in you. You, Lord, are forgiving and good, abounding in love to all who call to you.
PSALM 86:4–5 NIV

Forgiveness doesn't require that the person who did the hurting apologize or acknowledge what they've done. It's not about making the score even. It doesn't even require forgetting about the incident. But it is about admitting that the one who hurt us is human just like we are. We surrender our right for revenge and, like God, let go and give the wrongdoer mercy, therefore blessing them.

Gracious and loving Father, thank You that You love me and have forgiven me of my sins. May I be more like You in forgiving others. Although I may not be able to forgive as easily as You do, please encourage me to take those small steps. In forgiving others, Father, I am that much closer to being like You. Amen.

Divine Imaginings and Sublime Aspirations

He has made everything beautiful in its time.
He has also set eternity in the human heart.
ECCLESIASTES 3:11 NIV

Let's join hands. Let's celebrate. God has made everything beautiful in its time. He has also set eternity in the human heart. Never sit in the gutter when the steps of paradise are at your feet! So, widen your scope. See beauty in all things great and small. Soar free. Imagine beyond the ordinary. Love large. Forgive lavishly. Hope always. Expect a miracle.

Father, give me a contagious enthusiasm for life.
You have given me everything I need. Amen.

Which Way Do I Go?

I will instruct you and teach you in the way you should
go; I will counsel you with my loving eye on you.
PSALM 32:8 NIV

God says, "I will instruct you and teach you in the way you should go; I will counsel you with my loving eye on you." That is truly what we need in a noisy world that may offer little reliable or usable advice. God not only promises to guide us and teach us the way we should go, He plans on doing it with a loving eye on us. For the most loving counsel, listen to the voice of God. He's talking to you, and He has something important to say that will change your life.

Wonderful Counselor, help me to be receptive to Your
voice and to always trust in Your guidance. Amen.

DAY 225
Love Song of Forgiveness

*"In that day," declares the Lord, "you will call me
'my husband'; you will no longer call me 'my master.'"*
HOSEA 2:16 NIV

God wants *our* hearts. He desires a relationship with us
based on love and forgiveness. He enters into a covenant
with us, like the marriage between Hosea and Gomer.
God is the loving, faithful husband, constantly pursuing
us no matter what we do or where we roam. Though it
is difficult to grasp how much He loves us, we find hope
in His promise. God will keep His commitment to us.
His love song to us is forgiveness, and His wedding
vow is unconditional love.

*Thank You for loving me so fully and unconditionally,
God. I find comfort knowing that as much as any man
on earth could love me, You love me more. Amen.*

Hide and Seek

"Are you seeking great things for yourself? Don't do it! I will bring great disaster upon all these people."
JEREMIAH 45:5 NLT

God warns us: *Don't seek great things.* The more we seek them, the more elusive they become. As soon as we think we have them in our grasp, they disappear. If we commit to more activities than we can realistically handle, the best result is that we can't follow through. Worse, we might make them our gods. Jesus tells us what we should seek: the kingdom of God and His righteousness (Matthew 6:33). When we seek the right things, He'll give us every good and perfect gift (James 1:17). And that will be more than we can ask or dream.

Lord, please teach me to seek You, not personal greatness. May You be the all in all of my life. Amen.

God Is Doing Something New

"See, I am doing a new thing! Now it springs up;
do you not perceive it? I am making a way in the
wilderness and streams in the wasteland."

ISAIAH 43:19 NIV

Imagine that desert, dry and barren—with no hope of even a cactus flower to bloom—suddenly coming to life with bubbling pools of pure water. That is what God promises us. He is doing something new in our lives. He is making a path through what feels impass-able, and He will command a stream to flow through the wilderness of our pasts, places where we had only known the wasteland of sin and a landscape of despair. Have faith and bring your empty buckets to the stream.

Father, thank You for Your provision, hope,
and joy. Without You, life is dry and hostile.
Come into my life and quench my thirst.
You are the only one who can fulfill me. Amen.

How Should I Talk to God?

"This, then, is how you should pray:
'Our Father in heaven, hallowed be your
name, your kingdom come, your will be done,
on earth as it is in heaven. Give us today our
daily bread. And forgive us our debts, as we also
have forgiven our debtors. And lead us not into
temptation, but deliver us from the evil one.'"
MATTHEW 6: 9–13 NIV

Jesus gave us an example of how to pray in His famous
petition that was recorded in Matthew 6:9–13. We don't
need to suffer with an anxious heart or feel ensnared
by this world with no one to hear our cry for help. We
can talk to God right now, and He will listen. The act
of prayer is as simple as launching a boat into the Sea
of Galilee, but it's as miraculous as walking on water.

God, how wonderful it is that You hear me
when I call out to You and that You answer
with exactly what I need. Amen.

Only Believe

While Jesus was still speaking, some people came from the house of Jairus, the synagogue ruler. "Your daughter is dead," they said. "Why bother the teacher anymore?"
MARK 5:35 NIV

When the odds are stacked against us and circumstances riddle us with hopelessness, our tendency is to manage our burdens as well as we can and stop praying. Doubtful, we wonder: Can God restore an unhappy marriage? Can He heal cancer? Can He deliver me from financial ruin? *Will* He?

Jesus knows the way out. Only believe; have faith in Him and never lose hope.

Jesus, my hope is in You. Even when it appears that all hope is lost, I will hold on to the hope that You will deliver me. Amen.

Location, Location, Location

Those who live in the shelter of the Most High will find rest in the shadow of the Almighty. This I declare about the LORD: he alone is my refuge, my place of safety; he is my God, and I trust him.
PSALM 91:1–2 NLT

If something is getting you down in life, check your location. Where are your thoughts? Let what the world has conditioned you to think go in one ear and out the other. Stand on the truth, the promises of God's Word. Say of the Lord, "God is my refuge! I am hidden in Christ! Nothing can harm me. In Him I trust!" Say it loud. Say it often. Say it over and over until it becomes your reality. And you will find yourself dwelling in that secret place every moment of the day.

God, You are my refuge. When I abide in You, nothing can harm me. Your Word is the truth on which I rely. Fill me with Your light and the peace of Your love. It's You and me, Lord, all the way! Amen.

Jungle of Life

The word of God is alive and powerful. It is sharper than the sharpest two-edged sword, cutting between soul and spirit, between joint and marrow. It exposes our innermost thoughts and desires.

HEBREWS 4:12 NLT

When you take the Bible and live according to God's plans, obeying Him, God's Word cuts like a machete through the entanglements of life. When you choose to use the sword of truth, it clears a path and can free you from the weights of the world that try to entrap and ensnare you. No matter what the challenges of life are saying to you today, take His Word and speak His plans into your life. Choose His words of encouragement and peace instead of the negative things life's circumstances are telling you.

God, I want to live in Your truth. I want to believe what You say about me in the Bible. Help me to speak Your words today instead of the problem. Help me believe. Amen.

O the Deep, Deep Love of Jesus

I pray that out of his glorious riches he may strengthen you with power through his Spirit in your inner being, so that Christ may dwell in your hearts through faith. And I pray that you, being rooted and established in love, may have power, together with all the Lord's holy people, to grasp how wide and long and high and deep is the love of Christ.

EPHESIANS 3:16–18 NIV

What an amazing picture! That He should care for us in such a way is almost incomprehensible. Despite our shortcomings, our sin, He loves us. It takes a measure of faith to believe in His love. When we feel a nagging thought of unworthiness, of being unlovable, trust in the Word and sing a new song. For His love is deep and wide.

---

*Lord, thank You for loving me,
even when I'm unlovable. Amen.*

DAY 233
He Will Come

Do not snatch your word of truth from me,
for your regulations are my only hope.
PSALM 119:43 NLT

Bibles wear and tear. Papers get discarded. Hard drives crash. But memorizing scripture assures us that God's Word will never be lost. His truth will always be at our disposal, any moment of the day or night when we need a word of encouragement, of guidance, of hope. Like a phone call from heaven, our Father communicates to us via scripture implanted in our hearts. But it is up to us to build the signal tower.

Your Word is a never-ending source of hope in my life. When troubles come, I find comfort, peace, strength, love—whatever my soul thirsts for, I know I will find it in the Bible. Amen.

Laugh a Rainbow

*"When I see the rainbow in the clouds, I will
remember the eternal covenant between God
and every living creature on earth."*
GENESIS 9:16 NLT

Ever feel like a cloud is hanging over your head?
Sometimes the cloud darkens to the color of bruises,
and we're deluged with cold rain that seems to have
no end. When you're in the midst of one of life's thun-
derstorms, tape this saying to your mirror: cry a river;
laugh a rainbow. The rainbow, the symbol of hope that
God gave Noah after the flood, reminds us even today
that every storm will eventually pass.

---

*The rainbows you place in the sky after a storm
are lovely reminders of the hope we have in You,
God. Because of You, I know that the storms
of life are only temporary. . .and that You will
bring beauty from the storms. Amen.*

Seeking God's Plan

*For we are His workmanship, created in Christ
Jesus for good works, which God prepared
beforehand that we should walk in them.*

Ephesians 2:10 nkjv

How can you know God's plans for your life? First,
you should meet with Him in prayer each day and seek
His will. Studying the Bible is also important. Often,
God speaks to us directly through His Word (Psalm
119:105). Finally, you must have faith that God *will*
work out His plan for your life and that His plan is
good. Jeremiah 29:11 (niv) says, "For I know the plans
I have for you,' declares the Lord, 'plans to prosper
you and not to harm you, plans to give you hope and a
future.'" Are you living in Christ's example and seeking
God's plan for your life?

---

*Father, what is Your plan for me? I know that
it is good. Reveal it to me, Lord. Speak to me
through prayer and Your Word. Amen.*

Light My Path

Your word is a lamp for my feet, a light on my path.
PSALM 119:105 NIV

God's Word is like a streetlamp. Often, we *think* we know where we're going and where the stumbling blocks are. We believe we can avoid pitfalls and maneuver the path successfully on our own. But the truth is that without God's Word, we are walking in darkness, stumbling and tripping. When we sincerely begin to search God's Word, we find that the path becomes clear. God's light allows us to live our lives in the most fulfilling way possible, a way planned out from the very beginning by God Himself.

Jesus, shine Your light upon my path. I have spent too long wandering through the darkness, looking for my way. As I search Your Word, I ask You to make it a lamp to my feet so that I can avoid the pitfalls of the world and walk safely along the path You have created specifically for me. Amen.

DAY 237
The End of Your Rope

*Do not be far from me, for trouble is
near and there is no one to help.*
PSALM 22:11 NIV

Jesus reaches down and wraps you in His loving arms
when you call to Him for help. The Bible tells us that
He is close to the brokenhearted (Psalm 34:18). You may
not have the answers you are looking for here in this
life, but you can be sure of this: God sees your pain and
loves you desperately. Call to Him in times of trouble.
If you feel that you're at the end of your rope, look up!
His mighty hand is reaching toward you.

---

*Heavenly Father, I feel alone and afraid. Surround
me with Your love, and give me peace and joy. Amen.*

DAY 238
Fill 'Er Up

"What strength do I have, that I should still hope?"
JOB 6:11 NIV

Run, rush, hurry, dash: a typical American woman's day. It's easy to identify with David's lament in Psalm 22:14 (NASB): "I am poured out like water. . .my heart is like wax; it is melted within me." Translation: "I'm pooped; I'm numb; I'm drained dry." When we are at the end of our strength, God doesn't want us to lose hope of the refilling He can provide if we only lift our empty cups to Him.

Fill me up, Lord! I need Your heavenly presence. . .Your strength. . .Your comfort. Thank You for the hope You provide each day of my life! Amen.

Good News

Make the most of every opportunity in these evil days.
EPHESIANS 5:16 NLT

While it may seem tempting to crawl back into bed and hide beneath the covers of denial instead of facing the harsh reality of the world, God has a different idea. Every minute counts because we, as believers, carry an eternal hope that the world needs to hear. Bad things do happen to good people, but ever-present in the trials of this world is a loving God who cares deeply for His children. Who will you share this good news with today?

Dear God, how should I share the good news with those who have suffered at the hand of evil? Show me ways to encourage them that You love and care for them. Amen.

Power Up

*The Spirit of God, who raised Jesus
from the dead, lives in you.*
ROMANS 8:11 NLT

God is the same yesterday, today, and forever. His strength does not diminish over time. That same mountain-moving power you read about in the lives of people from the Old and New Testaments still exists today. We don't have to go it alone. Our heavenly Father wants to help. All we have to do is ask. He has already made His power available to His children. Whatever we face, wherever we go, whatever dreams we have for our lives, take courage and know that anything is possible when we draw on the power of God.

*Father, help me to remember that You are always
with me, ready to help me do all things. Amen.*

Refreshment in Dry Times

"The grass withers and the flowers fall,
but the word of our God endures forever."
ISAIAH 40:8 NIV

Sometimes our lives feel just like the grass—dry and listless. Maybe we're in a season where things seem to stand still, and we've tried everything to change our circumstances for the better to no avail. It is during those times that we need to remember the faithfulness of God and the permanence of His Word. His promises to us are many and true! God will never leave us or forsake us; and He will provide for, love, and protect us. And, just like the drought, eventually our personal dry times will give way to a time of growth, refreshment, and beauty.

Dear Lord, help me to remember Your love during
difficult times of dryness. Please remind me of Your
many promises, and remind me to stand firmly
on them. You are everything I need. Amen.

Power-Packed and Personal

Thou hast magnified thy word above all thy name.
PSALM 138:2 KJV

Of all the wonderful graces and gifts God has given humankind, there's nothing that touches the power and truth of that all-time bestseller, the Bible. The Bible provides healing, hope, and direction (Psalm 107:20; 119:74, 133). If we want wisdom and the desire to do things the right way, God's Word equips us (2 Timothy 3:16–17). From the scriptures, we can make sense of a confusing world. We can get a hold on real truth. God has given us His eternal Word to know Him and to know ourselves better.

Teach me not only to read but also to obey Your living, powerful Word every day, Lord God. Amen.

Releasing Your Hold on Anxiety

Search me, God, and know my heart; test me and know my anxious thoughts. See if there is any offensive way in me, and lead me in the way everlasting.

PSALM 139:23–24 NIV

What is it that weighs you down? Financial issues? An unhealthy relationship? Your busy schedule? Surrender these misgivings to a God who wants to take them from you. Ask Him to search your heart for any and all anxieties, for any and all signs that you have not truly put your trust in Him. Find the trouble spots in your life to which you direct most of your thoughts and energy, and then hand these troubles over to one who can truly address them. Realize that you are only human and that God is infinitely more capable of balancing your cares than you are.

Lord, take from me my anxieties, big and small. May I remember to give these to You daily so that I will not find myself distracted by the things of this world. Amen.

Behind the Scenes

*Now faith is confidence in what we hope for
and assurance about what we do not see.*
HEBREWS 11:1 NIV

Be encouraged today that no matter what takes place
in the natural—what you see with your eyes—it doesn't
have to be the final outcome of your situation. If you've
asked God for something, then you can trust that He
is working out all the details behind the scenes. What
you see right now, how you feel, is not a picture of what
your faith is producing. Your faith is active, and God
is busy working to make all things come together and
benefit you.

---

*Heavenly Father, what I see today is not what I'm
going to get. Thank You for working behind the scenes
to bring about the very best for my life. Amen.*

Comfort Food

*For whatever things were written before were
written for our learning, that we through the patience
and comfort of the Scriptures might have hope.*
ROMANS 15:4 NKJV

Romans 15:4 tells us that the scriptures are comfort food for the soul. They were written and given so that through our learning, we would be comforted with the truths of God. Worldly pleasures bring a temporary comfort, but the problem still remains when the pleasure or comfort fades. However, the words of God are soothing and provide permanent hope and peace. Through God's Word, you will be changed, and your troubles will dim in the bright light of Christ. So the next time you are sad, lonely, or disappointed, turn to the Word of God as your source of comfort.

*Thank You, Father, for the rich comfort Your
Word provides. Help me to remember to find my
comfort in scripture rather than through earthly
things that will ultimately fail me. Amen.*

Praying the Mind of Christ

We demolish arguments and every pretension that sets itself up against the knowledge of God, and we take captive every thought to make it obedient to Christ.
2 CORINTHIANS 10:5 NIV

By reading and praying scripture and using positive statements in our prayers that claim what God has already said He will do for us, the mind of Christ is being activated in us. By taking captive every thought, we learn to know what thought is of God, what belongs to us, and what is of the enemy. Recognize, take captive, and bind up the thoughts that are of the enemy and throw them out! The more we commune with God, fellowship with Him, and learn from Him, the more we cultivate the mind of Christ.

Lord, help me identify the thoughts that are not Your thoughts and purge them. Then I will hear You more clearly so I may be an obedient disciple. Amen!

Aim High

*My aim is to raise hopes by pointing
the way to life without end.*
TITUS 1:2 MSG

No woman is an island. We're more like peninsulas. Although we sometimes feel isolated, we're connected to one another by the roots of womanhood. We're all in this together, girls. As we look around, we can't help but see sisters who need a hand, a warm smile, a caring touch. . .and especially hope. People need hope, and if we know the Lord— the source of eternal hope—it's up to us to point the way through love.

---

*I have so many women in my life who are
constant reminders of the one eternal source of
hope—YOU, Father God. Thank You for placing
these beautiful women in my life. Amen.*

Easy as ABC

*"His purpose was for the nations to seek after God
and perhaps feel their way toward him and find
him—though he is not far from any one of us."*
ACTS 17:27 NLT

God is near. . .but we must reach out for Him. There's
a line that we choose to cross, a specific action we take.
We can't ooze into the kingdom of God; it's an inten-
tional decision. It's simple, really—as simple as ABC.
A is Admitting we're sinful and in need of a Savior. *B*
is Believing that Jesus died for our sins and rose from
the grave. *C* is Committing our lives to Him. Life
everlasting is then ours.

---

*God, You are always within reach.
For that, I am so very thankful. I look forward
to eternal life in You presence. Amen.*

Standing Still

"The LORD will fight for you; you need only to be still."
EXODUS 14:14 NIV

Moses commanded the Israelites to stop panicking and stand still. Then God held back the waters of the Red Sea, and the Israelites were able to walk across on dry ground! When the Egyptians tried to follow them, the waters rushed in and drowned them all. Sometimes when we stress and panic, we rack our brains trying to figure out solutions to our problems; and instead of standing still and praying to God, we become even more panicked. Moses' words still apply to us today. When we face our fears, we should be still, trusting in God and relying on Him to bring us through the struggle.

Dear Lord, please teach me to be still and to trust in You. Thank You for Your constant faithfulness. Amen.

Power of the Word

*"The Spirit gives life; the flesh counts for
nothing. The words I have spoken to you—
they are full of the Spirit and life."*
JOHN 6:63 NIV

Jesus told His followers that His words were Spirit and
life. When we hear His Word, meditate on it, pray it,
memorize it, and ask for faith to believe it, He comes
to us in it and transforms our lives through it. Once the
Word is in our minds or before our eyes and ears, the
Holy Spirit can work it into our hearts and our con-
sciences. Jesus told us to abide in His Word. . .putting
ourselves in a place to hear and receive the Word. The
rest is the beautiful and mysterious work of the Spirit.

---

*Thank You, Jesus, the living Word,
for changing my heart and my mind through
the power of Your Word. Amen.*

Snippets of Hope

*I also pray that you will understand the incredible
greatness of God's power for us who believe him.*
EPHESIANS 1:19 NLT

Daydreams are snippets of hope for our souls—
yearnings for something better, something more exciting, something that lifts our spirits. Some dreams are
mere fancy, but others are meant to last a lifetime
because God embedded them in our hearts. It's when
we lose sight of those dreams that hope dies. But God
offers us access to His almighty power—the very same
greatness that brought His Son back from the dead.
What greater hope is there?

*Thank You for the dreams you wove into my
heart, Father God. Please help me keep those
dreams for the future alive. Amen.*

Makeover

I was shown mercy so that in me, the worst of sinners, Christ Jesus might display his immense patience as an example for those who would believe in him and receive eternal life.

1 TIMOTHY 1:16 NIV

Saul was a Jesus-hater. He went out of his way to hunt down believers to torture, imprison, and kill. Yet, Christ tracked him down and confronted him in a blinding light on a dusty road. Saul's past no longer mattered. Previous sins were forgiven and forgotten. He was given a fresh start. A life makeover. We too are offered a life makeover. Christ offers to create a beautiful new image of Himself in us, unblemished and wrinkle-free.

Thank You for new beginnings and fresh starts, God. You have erased my sins, and now I walk free in Your unending grace! Amen.

The Blues

*Why, my soul, are you downcast? Why so
disturbed within me? Put your hope in God,
for I will yet praise him, my Savior and my God.*
PSALM 42:11 NIV

Everyone experiences times when frustrations seem to outweigh joy, but as Christians, we have an unending source of encouragement in God. *That's great,* you may think, *but how am I supposed to tap into that joy?* First, pray. Ask God to unburden your spirit. Share your stress, frustrations, and worries with Him. Don't hold back; He can take it. Make a list of the blessings in your life and thank the Provider of those blessings. Choose to not focus on yourself; instead, praise Him for being Him. Soon you'll feel true, holy refreshment—the freedom God wants you to live out every day.

---

*Rejuvenate my spirit, Lord! You alone can
take away the burden I feel. You are my
hope and my redeemer forever. Amen.*

Can God Interrupt You?

In their hearts humans plan their course,
but the LORD establishes their steps.
PROVERBS 16:9 NIV

Have you ever considered that perhaps God has ordained our interruptions? Perhaps, just perhaps, God may be trying to get your attention. There is nothing wrong with planning our day. However, we have such limited vision. God sees the big picture. Be open. Be flexible. Allow God to change your plans in order to accomplish His divine purposes. Instead of becoming frustrated, look for ways the Lord might be working. Be willing to join Him. When we do, interruptions become blessings.

Dear Lord, forgive me when I am so rigidly
locked into my own agenda that I miss Yours.
Give me Your eternal perspective so that I may
be open to divine interruptions. Amen.

DAY 255
Standing in the Light

*Though I have fallen, I will rise. Though I sit
in darkness, the LORD will be my light.*
MICAH 7:8 NIV

We may fall down, but God will lift us up. We may feel
surrounded by darkness on every side, but He will be
our light, guiding the way, showing us which step to
take next. No matter where we are, what we've done, or
what we're facing, God is our rescuer, our Savior, and
our friend. Satan wants to convince us that we have no
hope, no future. But God's children always have a future
and a hope; we are cherished, and we belong to Him.

---

*Dear Father, thank You for giving me confidence in
a future filled with good things. When I'm down,
remind me to trust in Your love. Thank You for lifting
me out of darkness to stand in Your light. Amen.*

Sprouts

"For there is hope for a tree, when it is cut down, that it will sprout again."
JOB 14:7 NASB

Have you ever battled a stubborn tree—you know, one you can saw off at the ground but the tenacious thing keeps sprouting new growth from the roots? You have to admire the resiliency of that life force, struggling in its refusal to give up. That's hope in a nutshell, sisters. We must believe, even as stumps, that we will eventually become majestic, towering evergreens if we just keep sending out those sprouts.

Father God, help me continue to hope that I will grow into the woman You created me to be—just like the majestic, towering evergreen. Amen.

DAY 257
Home

*"But we will devote ourselves to prayer
and to the ministry of the word."*
ACTS 6:4 NASB

As busy women, we've found out the hard way that we can't do everything. Heaven knows we've tried, but the truth has found us out: superwoman is a myth. So, we must make priorities and focus on the most important. Prayer and God's Word should be our faith priorities. If we only do as much as we can do, then God will take over and do what only He can do. He's got our backs, girls!

I know I can't do it all, God. I find comfort in knowing that if I put my faith in You wholeheartedly, You will always help me prioritize my to-do list and get the R & R I need. Amen.

Rock Solid

"Therefore everyone who hears these words of mine and puts them into practice is like a wise man who built his house on the rock. The rain came down, the streams rose, and the winds blew and beat against that house; yet it did not fall, because it had its foundation on the rock."

MATTHEW 7:24–25 NIV

Prepare for tomorrow's storms by laying a solid foundation today. Rain and wind are guaranteed to come. It is only a matter of time. We need to be ready. When our foundation is the Rock, Jesus Christ, we will find ourselves still standing after the storm has passed. Rain will come. Winds will blow and beat hard against us. Yet, when our hope is in the Lord, we will not be destroyed. We will remain steadfast because our feet have been firmly planted. Stand upon the Rock today so that your tomorrows will be secure.

Dear Lord, help me build my foundation today upon You so I can remain steadfast in the storms of life. Amen.

Marvelous Thunder

"God's voice thunders in marvelous ways;
he does great things beyond our understanding."
JOB 37:5 NIV

Have you ever reflected deeply on the power that God is? Not that He *has*, but that He is. Consider this: The one who controls nature also holds every one of our tears in His hand. He is our Father, and He works on our behalf. He is more than enough to meet our needs; He does things far beyond what our human minds can understand. This one who is power loves you. He looks at you and says, "I delight in you, My daughter." Wow! His ways are marvelous and beyond understanding.

Lord God, You are power. You hold all
things in Your hand and You chose to love me.
You see my actions, hear my thoughts, watch my
heartbreak. . .and You still love me. Please help
me trust in Your power, never my own. Amen.

Loving the Unlovable

*"You have heard the law that says, 'Love your neighbor'
and hate your enemy. But I say, love your enemies!
Pray for those who persecute you! In that way, you will
be acting as true children of your Father in heaven."*
MATTHEW 5:43–45 NLT

Sometimes running into a difficult person can actually
be a divine appointment! Maybe you're the only person
they'll see all week who wears a smile on her face. When
you happen upon a difficult person whom you'd rather
not talk to, take the time to pray about your attitude
and then pray for that person. Greet them with a smile
and look them in the eye. There is no reason to fear
difficult people if you trust in God. He will show you
what to do and say as you listen to His promptings
(Luke 12:12).

*Heavenly Father, I pray that You would help
me not to shy away from the people You have
allowed to cross my path. Help me speak Your
truth and share Your love boldly. Amen.*

Up Is the Only Out

Let them lie face down in the dust,
for there may be hope at last.
<small>LAMENTATIONS 3:29 NLT</small>

The Old Testament custom for grieving people was to lie prostrate and cover themselves with ashes. Perhaps the thought was that when you're wallowing in the dust, at least you can't descend any farther. There's an element of hope in knowing that there's only one way to go: up. If a recent loss has you sprawled in the dust, know that God doesn't waste pain in our lives. He will use it for some redeeming purpose.

Help me to recognize the purpose in my pain, Father.
I know You have a plan for my life—and that
Your plans are good. I trust You, Father. Amen.

Do a Little Dance

*Then Miriam. . .took a tambourine and led all the
women as they played their tambourines and danced.*
EXODUS 15:20 NLT

Can you imagine the enormous celebration that broke
out among the children of Israel after God miraculously
saved them from Pharaoh's army? Even dignified
prophetess Miriam grabbed her tambourine and cut
loose with her girlfriends. Despite adverse circumstances, she heard God's music and did His dance. Isn't
that our goal today? To hear God's music above the
world's cacophony and do His dance as we recognize
everyday miracles in our lives?

---

*Make me aware of Your everyday miracles,
Father. Help me to listen closely for Your
music so I can join in the dance. Amen.*

God's Work

*The LORD will perfect that which concerns
me; Your mercy, O LORD, endures forever;
do not forsake the works of Your hands.*
PSALM 138:8 NKJV

The psalmist offers hope when he tells us the Lord
will complete things that concern us. We are the work
of His hands, and He has enduring mercy toward our
failures. He is as active in our sanctification as He is
in our salvation. Philippians 1:6 (NKJV) says, "Being
confident of this very thing, that He who has begun
a good work in you will complete it until the day of
Jesus Christ." The power to change or to see difficult
things through to the end comes from the Lord, who
promises to complete the work He begins.

---

*Lord, remind me of this word when I
am discouraged by my lack of progress.
Help me remember Your eternal love
and mercy to me. Give me confidence
that You will complete me. Amen.*

Eye Care

For thus says the LORD of hosts: ". . .He who
touches you touches the apple of His eye."
ZECHARIAH 2:8 NKJV

To think that we are the apple of God's eye is incredible.
Consider the care He must take for us. He will go to
great lengths to protect us from harm. When something or someone does attack us, God feels our pain.
He is instantly aware of our discomfort, for it is His
own. When the storms of life come, we must remember
that God feels each twinge of suffering. Despite the
adversity, we can praise God, for He is sheltering us.

Thank You, God, that You are so aware of what is
happening to me. Thank You for Your protection. Amen.

Pebbles

*"I will give you a new heart and put a new spirit
within you; and I will remove the heart of stone
from your flesh and give you a heart of flesh."*
 EZEKIEL 36:26 NASB

So many things can harden our hearts: overwhelming
loss; shattered dreams; even scar tissue from broken
hearts, disillusionment, and disappointment. To avoid
pain, we simply turn off feelings. Our hearts become
petrified rock—heavy, cold, and rigid. But God can crack
our hearts of stone from the inside out and replace that
miserable pile of pebbles with soft, feeling hearts of flesh.
The amazing result is a brand-new, hope-filled spirit.

---

*God, please take my hard heart and make it
soft again. Renew my spirit with Your hope.
Transform me from the inside out! Amen.*

Permission to Mourn

When I heard this, I sat down and wept. In fact, for days
I mourned, fasted, and prayed to the God of heaven.
NEHEMIAH 1:4 NLT

Bad news. When it arrives, what's your reaction? Do you scream? Fall apart? Run away? Nehemiah's response to bad news is a model for us. First, he vented his sorrow. It's okay to cry and mourn. Christians suffer pain like everyone else—only we know the source of inner healing. Disguising our struggle doesn't make us look more spiritual—just less real. Like Nehemiah, our next step is to turn to the only true source of help and comfort.

Thank You for being big enough, God, to carry my sorrow. I am thankful that with You, I can always be real. . .sharing my every thought and emotion. And You love me still! Amen.

Take Heart

"In this world you will have trouble.
But take heart! I have overcome the world."
JOHN 16:33 NIV

Christ tells us to hold on to the hope we have in Him. He tells us to "take heart" because the trials of this world have already been won, the evil has already been conquered, and He has already overcome the world. Live your life as a statement of hope, not despair. Live like the victor, not the victim. Live with your eye on eternity, not the here and now. Daily remind yourself that you serve a powerful and gracious God, and decide to be used by Him to act as a messenger of grace and healing to the world's brokenness.

Lord, forgive my doubts. Forgive me for growing
discouraged and not placing my full trust in
You. May I learn to trust You better and to
live my life as a statement of hope. Amen.

God's Mountain Sanctuary

And seeing the multitudes, he went up into a
mountain: and. . .his disciples came unto him:
and he opened his mouth, and taught them.
MATTHEW 5:1–2 KJV

Jesus often retreated to a mountain to pray. There He called His disciples to depart from the multitudes so that He could teach them valuable truths—the lessons we learn from nature. Do you yearn for a place where problems evaporate like the morning dew? Do you need a place of solace? God is wherever you are—behind a bedroom door, nestled alongside you in your favorite chair, or even standing at a sink full of dirty dishes. Come apart and enter God's mountain sanctuary.

Heavenly Father, I long to hear Your voice and to
flow in the path You clear before me. Help me to
find sanctuary in Your abiding presence. Amen.

Whispers in the Wind

*Then Jesus told him, "Because you have seen
me, you have believed; blessed are those who
have not seen and yet have believed."*

JOHN 20:29 NIV

We can't see God. We can't take Him by the hand or
even converse with Him face-to-face like we do a friend.
But we still know He is present in our lives because
we can experience the effects. God moves among His
people, and we can see it. God speaks to His people,
and we can hear the still, small voice. And, just like we
can feel the wind across our cheeks, we can feel God's
presence. We don't need to physically see God to know
that He exists and that He's working.

---

*You are like the wind, Lord. Powerful and fast moving,
soft and gentle. We may not see You, but we can sense
You. Help us to believe, even when we can't see. Amen.*

Feel the Love

*Long before he laid down earth's foundations,
he had us in mind, had settled on us as the focus of
his love, to be made whole and holy by his love.*
EPHESIANS 1:4 MSG

Need a boost of hope today? Read this passage aloud,
inserting your name for each "us." Wow! Doesn't that
bring home the message of God's incredible, extrava-
gant, customized love for you? I am the focus of His
love, and I bask in the hope of healing, wholeness, and
holiness His individualized attention brings. You too,
dear sister, are His focus. Allow yourself to feel the
love today.

*Long before You laid down earth's foundations,
You had me in mind, had settled on me as the
focus of Your love, to be made whole and holy
by Your love. Thank You, Jesus! Amen.*

DAY 271
Seeking an Oasis

*He turns a wilderness into a pool of water,
and a dry land into springs of water.*
PSALM 107:35 NASB

The wilderness of Israel is truly a barren wasteland—nothing but rocks and parched sand stretching as far as the distant horizon. The life-and-death contrast between stark desert and pools of oasis water is startling. Our lives can feel parched too. Colorless. Devoid of life. But God has the power to transform desert lives into gurgling, spring-of-water lives. Ask Him to bubble up springs of hope within you today.

---

*When I am feeling parched, Jesus, I trust You'll
create a peaceful oasis in my soul. Envelop
my spirit in Your hope, Lord. Amen.*

Rescued

*God rescued us from dead-end alleys and dark dungeons.
He's set us up in the kingdom of the Son he loves so
much, the Son who got us out of the pit we were in,
got rid of the sins we were doomed to keep repeating.*

COLOSSIANS 1:13–14 MSG

The message of the gospel doesn't leave us trapped in
our sin and misery without hope. God sent the rescuer,
Christ, who plucked us out of the dungeons of despair
and into His kingdom of light and strength to overcome
the dragons of sin. It's by the Father's grace that we
are not stuck in our habitual ruts and dead-end alleys,
living without purpose and fulfillment. We walk in His
kingdom—a kingdom that goes counter to the world's
ideas. We are out of the pit, striding confidently in Him,
enjoying life to its fullest.

---

*Glory to You, Jesus! You have rescued me from the
pit and lifted me to Your kingdom of real life and
victory. Help me to walk in that fact today. Amen.*

A Fragrant Offering

Follow God's example, therefore, as dearly loved children and walk in the way of love, just as Christ loved us and gave himself up for us as a fragrant offering and sacrifice to God.
EPHESIANS 5:1–2 NIV

If we carry the scent of Christ in our daily walk, people will be drawn to us and want to stay for a while. But how do we give off that amazing, inviting fragrance? There's really only one way—by imitating God. By loving others fully. By seeing them through His eyes. By looking with great compassion on those who are hurting, as Jesus did when He went about healing the sick and pouring out His life for those in need. As we live a life of love in front of those we care for, we exude the sweetest fragrance of all—Christ.

Dear Lord, I long to live a life that points people to You. As I care for those in need, may the sweet-smelling aroma of You and Your love be an invitation for people to draw near. Amen.

Cherished Desire

Now may our Lord Jesus Christ himself and God our Father, who loved us and by his grace gave us eternal comfort and a wonderful hope, comfort you and strengthen you in every good thing you do and say.
2 THESSALONIANS 2:16–17 NLT

Webster's definition of hope: "to cherish a desire with anticipation." In other words, yearning for something wonderful you expect to occur. Our hope in Christ is not just yearning for something wonderful, as in "I hope for a sunny beach day." It's a deep trust with roots that extend from the beginning of time to the infinite future. Our hope is not just the anticipation of heaven but the expectation of a fulfilling life walking beside our Creator and best Friend.

Dear heavenly Father, I want to journey through life in hopeful expectation—always anticipating You'll work in wonderful ways! Amen.

A New Tomorrow

*Rahab the prostitute. . . , Joshua spared. . .because she
hid the messengers whom Joshua sent to spy out Jericho.*
JOSHUA 6:25 NASB

Rahab was the unlikeliest of heroes: a prostitute who
sold her body in the darkest shadows. Yet, she was the
very person God chose to fulfill His prophecy. How
astoundingly freeing, especially for those of us ashamed
of our past. God loved Rahab for who she was—not
for what she did. Rahab is proof that God can and will
use anyone for His higher purposes. Anyone. Even you
and me.

---

*When I feel absolutely useless, God, remind me
of Rahab's story. If You could use Rahab for Your
purposes, You can certainly use me! Amen.*

Can You Hear Me Now?

But as for me, I watch in hope for the LORD,
I wait for God my Savior; my God will hear me.
MICAH 7:7 NIV

If there's anything more frustrating than waiting for someone who never shows, it's trying to talk to someone who isn't listening. It's as if they have plugged their ears and nothing penetrates. Mothers are well acquainted with this exercise in futility, as are wives, daughters, and sisters. But the Bible tells us that God hears us when we talk to Him. He shows up when we wait for Him. He will not disappoint us.

When I talk, Lord, I know You will listen.
You will never let me down. Amen.

Joyful, Patient, and Faithful

Be joyful in hope, patient in affliction, faithful in prayer.
ROMANS 12:12 NIV

Faithfulness in prayer requires discipline. God is faithful regardless of our attitude toward Him. He never changes, wavers, or forsakes His own. We may be faithful to do daily tasks around the house. We feed the cat, wash the clothes, and empty the trash. But faithfulness in the quiet discipline of prayer is harder. There are seemingly no consequences for neglecting our time with the Lord. Oh, what a myth this is! Set aside a daily time for prayer, and see how the Lord blesses you, transforming your spirit to increase your joyful hope, your patience, and your faithfulness.

Faithful God, find me faithful. Stir up hope and joy within me. Give me the grace I need to wait on You. Amen.

Masterpiece

*You made all the delicate, inner parts of my body
and knit me together in my mother's womb.*
PSALM 139:13 NLT

At the moment of your conception, roughly three million decisions were made about you. Everything from your eye color and the number of your wisdom teeth to the shape of your nose and the swirl of your fingerprints was determined in the blink of an eye. God is a big God. Unfathomable. Incomparable. Frankly, words just don't do Him justice. And He made *you*. You were knit together by a one-of-a-kind, amazing God who is absolutely, undeniably, head over heels, crazy in love with you. Try to wrap your brain around that.

---

*Heavenly Father and Creator, thank You for
the amazing gift of life, for my uniqueness
and individuality. Help me to use my life
as a gift of praise to You. Amen.*

Encourage Others

Worry weighs a person down;
an encouraging word cheers a person up.
PROVERBS 12:25 NLT

There is so much sorrow in this world. At any given time, there are many people within your sphere of influence who are hurting. Worry weighs them down as they face disappointment, loss, and other trials. Think about how much it means to you when someone takes the time to encourage you. Do the same for others. Be the voice of encouragement. There is blessing to be found in lifting up those around you.

Father, as I go through this week, make me an encourager. Provide opportunities for me to encourage those around me. I truly desire to cheer up the hearts of those who are worried. Amen.

DAY 280
Go for It

When everything was hopeless, Abraham
believed anyway, deciding to live. . .
on what God said he would do.
ROMANS 4:18 MSG

"You can't do that. It's impossible." Have you ever been told this—or just thought it because of fear or a previous experience with failure? This world is full of those who discourage rather than encourage. If we believe them, we'll never do anything. But if we, like Abraham, believe that God has called us for a particular purpose, we'll go for it despite our track records. Past failure doesn't dictate future failure. If God wills it, He fulfills it.

Help me to have the faith of Abraham,
Father God. . .to believe anyway! Amen.

Jets and Submarines

*No power in the sky above or in the earth below. . .
will ever be able to separate us from the love of
God that is revealed in Christ Jesus our Lord.*
ROMANS 8:39 NLT

Have you ever been diving amid the spectacular array of
vivid color and teeming life in the silent world under the
sea? Painted fish of rainbow hues are backlit by diffused
sunbeams. Multi-textured coral dot the gleaming white
sand. You honestly feel as if you're in another world. But
every world is God's world. He soars above the clouds
with us and spans the depths of the seas. Nothing can
separate us from His love.

---

*Your love amazes me, Father. Just when
I find myself questioning how You could
possibly love me so much, I am reminded of the
precious promises of Your Word. Amen.*

Unbroken Promise

In hope of eternal life which God,
who cannot lie, promised before time began.
TITUS 1:2 NKJV

God always keeps His word. The Bible is filled with the promises of God—vows to us that are guaranteed to be completed. God never lies. Lying is not in Him. He sees us as worthy of His commitment. The promise of eternal life—given even before time began—is one of God's most wonderful gifts. No matter how disappointed we are with ourselves or with others, we only have to look at the pledge God has made to be filled with a heart of praise and gladness.

God, thank You that Your Word is trustworthy and true. Praise You for the promise of eternal life. Amen.

How About Some Fun?

A twinkle in the eye means joy in the heart,
and good news makes you feel fit as a fiddle.
PROVERBS 15:30 MSG

God does not want His kids to be worn out and stressed out. A little relaxation, recreation—and yes—*fun* are essential components of a balanced life. Even Jesus and His disciples found it necessary to get away from the crowds and pressures of ministry to rest. There's a lot of fun to be had out there—playing tennis or golf, jogging, swimming, painting, knitting, playing a musical instrument, visiting an art gallery, playing a board game, or going to a movie, a play, or a football game. Have you had any fun this week?

Lord, You are the one who gives balance to
my life. Help me to find time today for a little
relaxation, recreation, and even fun. Amen.

The Simple Things

In him our hearts rejoice, for we trust in his holy name.
PSALM 33:21 NIV

God knows all the simple pleasures you enjoy—and He created them for your delight. When the simple things that can come only by His hand fill you with contentment, He is pleased. He takes pleasure in you. You are His delight. Giving you peace, comfort, and a sense of knowing that you belong to Him is a simple thing for Him. Take a moment today and step away from the busyness of life. Take notice and fully experience some of those things you enjoy most. Then share that special joy with Him.

Lord, thank You for the simple things that bring pleasure to my day. I enjoy each gift You've given me. I invite You to share those moments with me today. Amen.

Keep Breathing, Sister!

There is hope only for the living. As they say,
"It's better to be a live dog than a dead lion!"
ECCLESIASTES 9:4 NLT

Isn't this a tremendous scripture? At first glance, the ending elicits a chuckle. But consider the truth it contains: Regardless of how powerful, regal, or intimidating a lion is, when he's dead, he's dead. But the living—you and I—still have hope. Limitless possibilities! Hope for today and for the future. Although we may be as lowly dogs, fresh, juicy bones abound. As long as we're breathing, it's not too late!

God of possibilities, remind me that it's
never too late as long as I'm breathing.
Because of You, I have hope! Amen.

Remember This

*Keep your eyes on Jesus, who both began
and finished this race we're in.*
HEBREWS 12:2 MSG

When our heads are spinning and tears are flowing, there is only one thing to remember: focus on Jesus. He will never leave you nor forsake you. When you focus on Him, His presence envelops you. Where there is despair, He imparts hope. Where there is fear, He imparts faith. Where there is worry, He imparts peace. He will lead you on the right path and grant you wisdom for the journey. When the unexpected trials of life come upon you, remember this: focus on Jesus.

Dear Lord, I thank You that nothing takes You by surprise. When I am engulfed in the uncertainties of life, help me remember to focus on You. Amen.

Ladies in Waiting

I will wait for the LORD. . . . I will put my trust in him.
ISAIAH 8:17 NIV

Do we want joy without accepting heartache? Peace without living through the stress? Patience without facing demands? God sees things differently. He's giving us the opportunity to learn through these delays, irritations, and struggles. Like Isaiah, we need to learn the art of waiting on God. He will come through every time—but in *His* time, not ours. The wait may be hours or days, or it could be years. But God is always faithful to provide for us. It is when we learn to wait on Him that we will find joy, peace, and patience through the struggle.

Father, You know what I need, so I will wait. Help me be patient, knowing that You control my situation and that all good things come in Your time. Amen.

A Joyful Heart

*Sarah said, "God has brought me
laughter, and everyone who hears
about this will laugh with me."*
GENESIS 21:6 NIV

In the Bible, King Solomon said, "For the despondent, every day brings trouble; for the happy heart, life is a continual feast" (Proverbs 15:15 NLT). Are you or someone you know unhappy? A little laughter might help. Begin with a smile. When you hear laughter, move toward it and try to join in. Seek the company of happy friends, and invite humor into your conversations. Most of all, praise God. Praise is the best way to heal a hurting soul. Praise God joyfully for His many blessings.

*Lord, whenever my heart is heavy,
encourage me to heal it with joy. Amen.*

Unswerving Faith

Let us hold unswervingly to the hope we profess, for he who promised is faithful.
HEBREWS 10:23 NIV

The author of Hebrews challenges us to hold *unswervingly* to our hope in Christ Jesus. Certainly, we fail to do this at times, but life is much better when we keep our eyes fixed on Him. Sometimes just a whisper from Satan—the father of lies—can cause shakiness where once there was steadfastness. Place your hope in Christ alone. He will help you to resist the lies of this world. Hold *unswervingly* to your Savior today. He is faithful!

---

*Jesus, You are the object of my hope.
There are many distractions in my life, but I
pray that You will help me to keep my eyes on
You. Thank You for Your faithfulness. Amen.*

Small but Mighty

He has. . .exalted the humble.
LUKE 1:52 NLT

God delights in making small things great. He's in the business of taking scrap-heap people and turning them into treasures: Noah (the laughingstock of his city), Moses (stuttering shepherd turned national leader), David (smallest among the big and powerful), Sarah (old and childless), Mary (poor teenager), Rahab (harlot turned faith-filled ancestor of Jesus). So you and I can rejoice with hope! Let us glory in our smallness!

I feel so very small today, God. Please remind me that because I am Yours, I am worthy. And that's all that matters! Amen.

Smiling in the Darkness

The hopes of the godless evaporate.
JOB 8:13 NLT

Hope isn't just an emotion; it's a perspective, a discipline, a way of life. It's a journey of choice. We must learn to override those messages of discouragement, despair, and fear that assault us in times of trouble and press toward the light. Hope is smiling in the darkness. It's confidence that faith in God's sovereignty amounts to something. . .something life-changing, life-saving, and eternal.

Father God, help me smile through the darkness today. Thank You for hope. Amen.

Fix Your Thoughts on Truth

*And now, dear brothers and sisters, one final thing.
Fix your thoughts on what is true, and honorable,
and right, and pure, and lovely, and admirable. Think
about things that are excellent and worthy of praise.*

PHILIPPIANS 4:8 NLT

Dig through the scriptures and find truths from God's
Word to combat any false message that you may be
struggling with. Write them down and memorize them.
Here are a few to get started:

God looks at my heart, not my outward
appearance. (1 Samuel 16:7)

I am free in Christ. (1 Corinthians 1:30)

I am a new creation. (2 Corinthians 5:17)

The next time you feel negative thoughts creeping in,
pray for the Lord to replace the doubts and negativity
with His words of truth.

---

*Lord God, please help me focus on truth.
Set my mind and heart on You alone. Amen.*

Consider the Heavens

When I consider your heavens, the work of your fingers, the moon and the stars, which you have set in place, what is mankind that you are mindful of them, human beings that you care for them?
PSALM 8:3–4 NIV

Daughter of God, you are important to your heavenly Father, more important than the sun, the moon, and the stars. You are created in the image of God, and He cares for you. In fact, He cares so much that He sent His Son, Jesus, to offer His life as a sacrifice for your sins. The next time you look up at the heavens, the next time you ooh and aah over a majestic mountain or emerald waves crashing against the shoreline, remember that those things in all their splendor don't even come close to you—God's greatest creation.

Oh Father, when I look at everything You have created, I'm so overwhelmed with who You are. Who am I that You would think twice about me? And yet You do. You love me, and for that I'm eternally grateful! Amen.

Pray about Everything

The LORD directs the steps of the godly.
He delights in every detail of their lives.
PSALM 37:23 NLT

The Bible says that the Lord delights in every detail of His children's lives. Adult prayers don't have to be well ordered and formal. God loves hearing His children's voices, and no detail is too little or too dull to pray about. Tell God that you hope the coffeehouse will have your favorite pumpkin-spice latte on their menu. Ask Him to give you patience as you wait in line. Thank Him for how wonderful that coffee tastes! Get into the habit of talking with Him all day long, because He loves you and delights in all facets of your life.

Dear God, teach me to pray about everything
with childlike innocence and faith. Amen.

Lord of the Dance

Remember your promise to me; it is my only hope.
PSALM 119:49 NLT

The Bible contains many promises from God: He will protect us (Proverbs 1:33), comfort us (2 Corinthians 1:5), help in our times of trouble (Psalm 46:1), and encourage us (Isaiah 40:29). The word encourage comes from the root phrase "to inspire courage." Like an earthly father encouraging his daughter from backstage as her steps falter during her dance recital, our Papa God wants to inspire courage in us if we only look to Him.

Promise-Keeper, You are the one true source of courage. Thank You for Your promises and for giving me courage when I need it most. Amen.

What Riches Do You Possess?

*Command those who are rich. . .not to be arrogant
nor to put their hope in wealth, which is so
uncertain, but to put their hope in God, who richly
provides us with everything for our enjoyment.*
1 TIMOTHY 6:17 NIV

God desires to bless us with possessions we can enjoy.
But it displeases Him when His children strain to attain
riches in a worldly manner out of pride or a compulsion
to flaunt. Riches are uncertain, but faith in God to meet
our provisions is indicative of the pure in heart. Pride
diminishes the capacity for humility and trust in God.
We are rich indeed when our hope and faith are not in
what we have but in whom we trust.

---

*Heavenly Father, my hope is in You for my needs
and my desires. I surrender any compulsion
to attain earthly wealth; rather, may I be rich
in godliness and righteousness. Amen.*

The Dream Maker

"What no eye has seen, what no ear has heard,
and what no human mind has conceived"—
the things God has prepared for those who love him.
1 CORINTHIANS 2:9 NIV

Dreams, goals, and expectations are part of our daily lives. We have an idea of what we want and how we're going to achieve it. Disappointment can raise its ugly head when what we wanted—what we expected—doesn't happen like we thought it should or doesn't happen as fast as we planned. God knows the dreams He has placed inside of you. He created you and knows what you can do—even better than you know yourself. Maintain your focus—not on the dream but on the dream maker—and together you will achieve your dream.

God, thank You for putting dreams in my heart. I refuse to quit. I'm looking to You to show me how to reach my dreams. Amen.

Listening Closely

I will listen to what God the LORD says.
PSALM 85:8 NIV

Listening is a learned art, too often forgotten in the busyness of a day. The alarm clock buzzes; we hit the floor running, toss out a prayer or maybe sing a song of praise, grab our car keys, and are out the door. If only we'd slow down and let the heavenly Father's words sink into our spirits, what a difference we might see in our prayer life. This day, stop. Listen. See what God has in store for you.

Lord, how I want to surrender and seek Your will!
Please still my spirit and speak to me. Amen.

Increasing Visibility

"Where then is my hope?"
JOB 17:15 NIV

On hectic days when fatigue takes its toll and we feel like cornless husks, hope disappears. When hurting people hurt people and we're in the line of fire, hope vanishes. When ideas fizzle, efforts fail; when we throw the spaghetti against the wall and nothing sticks, hope seems lost. But we must remember it's only temporary. The mountaintop isn't gone just because it's obscured by fog. Visibility will improve tomorrow, and hope will rise.

God of Hope, I am thankful to know You. . .and to trust that because of You, hope will rise. Amen.

A Little Goes a Long Way

"The LORD our God has allowed a few
of us to survive as a remnant."
EZRA 9:8 NLT

Remnants. Useless by most standards, but God is in the business of using tiny slivers of what's left to do mighty things. Nehemiah rebuilt the fallen walls of Jerusalem with a remnant of Israel; Noah's three sons repopulated the earth after the flood; four slave boys—Daniel, Shadrach, Meshach, and Abednego—kept faith alive for an entire nation. When it feels as if bits and pieces are all that has survived of your hope, remember how much God can accomplish with remnants!

Father God, thank You for proving that there
is hope. . .even in the remnants! Amen.

Reality Check

*Instead, you must worship Christ as Lord of your life.
And if someone asks about your hope as a believer,
always be ready to explain it. But do this in a gentle and
respectful way. Keep your conscience clear. Then if people
speak against you, they will be ashamed when they see
what a good life you live because you belong to Christ.*
1 PETER 3:15–16 NLT

Every day we are being watched—both by the Father
and by the people around us. Our attitudes and speech
often are weighed against beliefs we profess and the
hope we claim. Take time to search your heart and your
motivations. If your speech and attitude aren't Christ-
centered, re-aim your heart to hit the mark.

Lord, help me to be a good representative for You. Amen.

A Heavenly Party

"I tell you that in the same way there will be more rejoicing in heaven over one sinner who repents than over ninety-nine righteous persons who do not need to repent."

LUKE 15:7 NIV

The Father threw you your very own party the moment you accepted His Son as your Savior. Did you experience a taste of that party from the response of your spiritual mentors here on earth? As Christians, we should celebrate with our new brothers and sisters in Christ every chance we get. If you haven't yet taken that step in your faith, don't wait! Heaven's party planners are eager to get your celebration started.

Father, I am so grateful that You rejoice in new Christians. Strengthen my desire to reach the lost while I am here on earth. Then, when I reach heaven, the heavenly parties will be all the sweeter! Amen.

Start Your Day with God

*In the morning, LORD, you hear my
voice; in the morning I lay my requests
before you and wait expectantly.*
PSALM 5:3 NIV

As you wake up in the morning, thank the Lord for a new day. Ask Him to control your thoughts and attitude as you make the bed. Thank Him for providing for you as you toast your bagel. Ask that your self-image be based on your relationship with Christ as you get dressed and brush your teeth. Continue to pray as you drive to work or school. Spend time in His Word throughout the day. Then end your day by thanking Him for His love and faithfulness.

---

*Dear Lord, thank You for the gift of
a new day. Help me be aware of Your
constant presence in my life. Amen.*

My Refuge

God is our refuge and strength,
always ready to help in times of trouble.
PSALM 46:1 NLT

What is your quiet place? The place you go to get away from the fray, to chill out, think, regroup, and gain perspective? Mine is a hammock nestled beneath a canopy of oaks in my backyard. . .nobody around but birds, squirrels, an occasional wasp, God, and me. There I can pour out my heart to my Lord, hear His comforting voice, and feel His strength refresh me. We all need a quiet place. God, our refuge, will meet us there.

Father, thank You for my special place. . .the place I love to go and spend time in Your presence. Amen.

DAY 305
Devotion

And I will walk at liberty: for I seek thy precepts.
PSALM 119:45 KJV

Being devoted to someone you love is one thing. Being devoted to doing something, like completing a project or following God's commandments, is quite another. It doesn't sound as passionate or pleasurable, but devoting yourself to do what God asks isn't a self-improvement program. It's a labor of love. Commitment is a way of expressing love, whether it's honoring your marriage vows or devoting yourself to doing what's right. Love is a verb, always in action, making invisible emotions visible.

Your Word tells me that Your burden is light, Lord. When I serve You out of love rather than duty, You fill my heart with joy and peace! I live my life to praise Your name. Amen.

Daybreak

"As your days, so shall your strength be."
DEUTERONOMY 33:25 NKJV

There are times in life when we feel that the night season we're facing will last forever and that a new morning will never come. For those particularly dark seasons of your life, you don't have to look to the east to find the morning star but, instead, find that morning star in your heart. Allow the hope of God's goodness and love to rekindle faith. With the passing of the night, gather your strength and courage. A new day is dawning and, with it, new strength for the journey forward. All that God has promised will be fulfilled.

*Heavenly Father, help me to hold tightly
to faith, knowing that in this situation,
daybreak is on its way. Amen.*

Choosing Wisely

Our mouths were filled with laughter.
PSALM 126:2 NIV

We women often plan perfect family events, only to find out how imperfectly things can turn out. The soufflé falls, the cat leaps onto the counter and licks the cheese ball, or little Johnny drops Aunt Martha's crystal gravy dish (full of gravy, of course). The Bible says that Sarah laughed at the most unexpected, traumatic time of her life—when God announced that she would have a baby at the age of ninety (Genesis 18:12). At this unforeseen turn of events, she could either laugh, cry, or run away screaming. She chose to laugh.

Lord, give us an extra dollop of grace and peace to laugh about unexpected dilemmas that pop up. . . and to remember that our reaction is a choice. Amen.

Your Heavenly Father

The faithful love of the LORD never ends!
His mercies never cease. Great is his faithfulness;
his mercies begin afresh each morning.
LAMENTATIONS 3:22–23 NLT

Regardless of your relationship with your earthly father, your heavenly Father loves you with an *unfailing love*. He is faithful to walk with you through the ups and downs of life. Remember that every day is a day to honor your heavenly Father. Begin and end today praising Him for who He is. Express thanksgiving. Present your requests to Him. Tell Him how much you love Him. God longs to be your Abba Father, a loving Daddy to you, His daughter!

Father, thank You for being a loving God,
my Abba Father, my Redeemer. Amen.

DAY 309
Finding Balance

Hope deferred makes the heart sick,
but when the desire comes, it is a tree of life.
PROVERBS 13:12 NKJV

Jesus is your hope! He stands a short distance away bidding you to take a walk on water—a step of faith toward Him. Let Him direct you over the rough waters of life, overcoming each obstacle one opportunity at a time. Don't look at the big picture in the midst of the storm, but focus on the one thing you can do at the moment to help your immediate situation—one step at a time.

Lord, help me not to concentrate on the
distractions but to keep my focus on which step
to take next in order to reach You. Amen.

Flourishing

"I will be like the dew to Israel; he will blossom like a lily. Like a cedar of Lebanon he will send down his roots; his young shoots will grow. His splendor will be like an olive tree, his fragrance like a cedar of Lebanon. People will dwell again in his shade; they will flourish like the grain, they will blossom like the vine."

HOSEA 14:5–7 NIV

These are lovely verses, filled with reasons to feel gratitude to God. In this passage of scripture, God promises to refresh us and make us blossom. He vows that we will grow both roots and branches, our lives spreading deeper and wider so that we have the ability to bless others. He tells us that blessing always spreads outward: not only will we blossom, we will also help others to blossom. Our lives will have meaning. We will be fruitful and creative, contributing to the kingdom of heaven here on earth.

Lord of love, thank You for all the many ways You bless me. My heart overflows with gratitude. Amen.

Anxiety Check!

*Do not be anxious about anything, but in
every situation, by prayer and petition,
with thanksgiving, present your requests to God.*
PHILIPPIANS 4:6 NIV

Checking to make sure we've locked the door, turned off the stove, and unplugged the curling iron just comes naturally. So why do we forget some of the bigger checks in life? Take anxiety, for instance. When was the last time you did an anxiety check? Days? Weeks? Months? Chances are, you're due for another. After all, we're instructed not to be anxious about anything. Instead, we're to present our requests to God with thanksgiving in our hearts. We're to turn to Him in prayer so that He can take our burdens. Once they've lifted, it's bye-bye anxiety!

Father, I get anxious sometimes, and I don't always remember to turn to You. In fact, I forget to check for anxiety at all. Today, I hand my anxieties to You. Thank You that I can present my requests to You. Amen.

Be Happy!

Blessed are those who act justly,
who always do what is right.
PSALM 106:3 NIV

In the world that we live in today, some might think that a bank error or a mistake on a bill in their favor would be justification for keeping the money without a word. But a true Christ follower would not look at these kinds of situations as good or fortunate events. Our happiness is in being honest, doing what is right, because that happiness is the promised spiritual reward. Because we want to be blessed by God, to be a happy follower of Him, we will seek to always do what is right.

Gracious and heavenly Father, thank You for Your blessings each and every day. I am thankful to be Your follower. When I am tempted to do something that would displease You, remind me that You will bless me if I act justly. My happiness will be a much better reward. In Your name, amen.

Granter of Dreams

Hope deferred makes the heart sick,
but a dream fulfilled is a tree of life.
PROVERBS 13:12 NLT

As a teenager, I dreamed of one day writing a book. But life intervened, and I became a wife, mother, occupational therapist, and piano teacher. My writing dream was shelved. Twenty-five years later, after my youngest chick flew the coop, God's still, small voice whispered, "It's time." Within five years, the granter of dreams delivered more than seventy articles and nine book contracts. What's your dream? Be brave and take the first step.

Heavenly Father, please give me courage so that I will have the confidence to take the first step in following the dreams You planted deep within my heart. Amen.

A Fresh New Harvest

Do not rejoice over me, my enemy;
when I fall, I will arise; when I sit in
darkness, the LORD will be a light to me.
MICAH 7:8 NKJV

The enemy of your soul wants you to consider each failure and dwell on the past, fully intending to rob you of your future. But God wants you to take that seed of hope that seems to have died and bury it in His garden of truth—trusting Him for a new harvest of goodness and mercy. Once you have buried that seed deep in the ground of God's love, it will grow and become a part of His destiny for your life.

Lord, help me not to focus on the past but to
look to You every step of the way. Amen.

Difficult People

*Do not turn your freedom into an opportunity for
the flesh, but serve one another through love.*
GALATIANS 5:13 NASB

Sometimes, like David, we need to turn our skirmishes
with others over to the Lord. Then, by using our weapons—God's Word and a steadfast faith—we need to
love and forgive others as God loves and forgives us.
Although we may not like to admit it, we have all said
and done some pretty awful things ourselves, making
the lives of others difficult. Yet, God has forgiven us *and*
continues to love us. So do the right thing. Pull your
feet out of the mire of unforgiveness, sidestep verbal
retaliation, and stand tall in the freedom of love and
forgiveness.

---

*The words and deeds of others have left me
wounded and bleeding. Forgiveness and love
seem to be the last things on my mind. Change
my heart, Lord. Help me to love and forgive
others as You love and forgive me. Amen.*

A Good Morsel

Taste and see that the LORD is good;
blessed is the one who takes refuge in him.
PSALM 34:8 NIV

The world gives the idea to nonbelievers that God isn't worth a taste. The world emphasizes a self-focus, while the Lord says to put others before self and to put God before all. In reality, walking and talking with God is the best thing you can do for yourself. Like so many foods that are good for us, all it requires is that first taste, a tiny morsel, which whets the appetite for more of Him. Then you can be open to all the goodness, all the fullness, of the Lord.

Lord, fill my cup to overflowing with Your
love so that it pours out of me in a way that
makes others want what I have. Amen.

Heart of Devotion

Preserve my soul; for I am holy: O thou my
God, save thy servant that trusteth in thee.
PSALM 86:2 KJV

The heart of devotion isn't duty. It's love. The deeper your love, the deeper your devotion. What does being devoted to God look like? It's characterized by a "God first," instead of "me first," mentality. While it's true that being devoted to God means you'll spend time with Him, it also means you'll give your time to others. Your love of God will spill over onto the lives of those around you. Your devotion to God is beneficial to everyone!

Thank You for loving me so well, Lord. I want to
follow You and serve You because You have shown
Your faithfulness and goodness to me. Amen.

Shouts of Joy

*He will yet fill your mouth with laughter
and your lips with shouts of joy.*
JOB 8:21 NIV

Do you remember the last time you laughed till you cried? For many of us, it's been far too long. Stress tends to steal our joy, leaving us humorless and oh-so-serious. But lightness and fun haven't disappeared forever. They may be buried beneath the snow of a long, wintery life season, but spring is coming. Laughter will bloom again, and our hearts will soar as our lips shout with joy. Grasp that hope!

Father God, thank You for the hope of joy. I know that because I trust in You, as sure as spring follows winter, joy will again bloom in my heart. Amen.

DAY 319

What If?

The LORD will keep you from all
harm—he will watch over your life.
PSALM 121:7 NIV

Feeling safe and secure rests not in the world or in other human beings but with God alone. He is a Christian's help and hope in every frightening situation. He promises to provide peace to everyone who puts their faith and trust in Him. What are you afraid of today? Allow God to encourage you. Trust Him to bring you through it and to give you peace.

Dear Lord, hear my prayers, soothe me with
Your words, and give me peace. Amen.

Weary Days

Why art thou cast down, O my soul? and why art thou disquieted in me? hope thou in God: for I shall yet praise him for the help of his countenance. O my God, my soul is cast down within me: therefore will I remember thee from the land of Jordan, and of the Hermonites, from the hill Mizar.

PSALM 42:5–6 KJV

Our willingness to speak with God at the day's beginning shows our dependence on Him. We can't make it alone. It is a comforting truth that God never intended for us to trek through the hours unaccompanied. He promises to be with us. He also promises His guidance and direction as we meet people and receive opportunities to serve Him. Getting started is as simple as removing our head from beneath the pillows and telling God, "Good morning."

Lord, refresh my spirit and give me joy for today's activities. Amen.

A Strong Heart

*Whom have I in heaven but you? And earth
has nothing I desire besides you. My flesh and
my heart may fail, but God is the strength
of my heart and my portion forever.*
PSALM 73:25–26 NIV

You don't have to be strong. In your weakness, God's strength shines through. And His strength surpasses anything you could produce, even on your best day. It's the same strength that spoke the heavens and the earth into existence. It's the same strength that parted the Red Sea. And it's the same strength that made the journey up the hill to the cross. So how do you tap into that strength? There's really only one way. Come into His presence. Spend some quiet time with Him. Allow His strong arms to encompass you. God is all you will ever need.

*Father, I feel so weak at times. It's hard just
to put one foot in front of the other. But I
know You are my strength. Invigorate me
with that strength today, Lord. Amen.*

A Continual Feast

The cheerful heart has a continual feast.
PROVERBS 15:15 NIV

Our choice of companions has much to do with our outlook. Negativity and positivity are both contagious. The writer of Proverbs says that a cheerful heart has a continual feast, so it's safe to assume that a grumpy heart will feel hungry and lacking instead of full. While God calls us to minister to those who are hurting, we can do so with discernment. Next time someone complains, ask them to pray with you about their concerns. Tell them a story of how you overcame negativity or repaired a relationship. You might help turn their day around!

God, help me be a positive influence on my friends and family. Give me wisdom and the unwavering hope that comes from Christ so that I may share Your joy with others. Amen.

Cultivating Beauty

Humans are satisfied with whatever looks good; GOD probes for what is good.
PROVERBS 16:2 MSG

Like many women, you probably enjoy looking nice when you go out for a special occasion. You want a hairstyle that flatters your face, clothes that fit well, and a little makeup to enhance your eyes and cheeks. God likes it when you feel good about your appearance. Still though, He cares more about the inner you. He wants to cultivate what's good about you socially, emotionally, mentally, and spiritually. Join with Him in cultivating the beauty that's inside you.

You created me in Your image, God, and I'm so thankful! Let the glow on my face and the twinkle in my eyes come from a heart that knows Your love and faithfulness. Amen.

Strength in the Lord

*The LORD is my light and my salvation—
whom shall I fear? The LORD is the stronghold
of my life—of whom shall I be afraid?*
PSALM 27:1 NIV

At times, this world can be a tough, unfair, lonely place. Since the fall of man in the garden, things have not been as God originally intended. The Bible assures us that we will face trials in this life, but it also exclaims that we are more than conquerors through Christ who is in us! When you find yourself up against a tribulation that seems insurmountable, *look up*. Christ is there. He goes before you, stands with you, and is backing you up in your time of need. You may lose everyone and everything else in this life, but nothing has the power to separate you from the love of Christ. Nothing.

---

*Jesus, I cling to the hope I have in You. You are
my rock, my stronghold, my defense. I will not
fear, for You are with me always. Amen.*

Bringing Us to Completion

*Being confident of this, that he who began
a good work in you will carry it on to
completion until the day of Christ Jesus.*
PHILIPPIANS 1:6 NIV

No matter how many times we fail, no matter how many times we mess up, we know God hasn't written us off. He's still working on us. He still loves us. Those of us who have been adopted into God's family through believing in His Son, Jesus Christ, can be confident that God won't give up on us. No matter how messed up our lives may seem, He will continue working in us until His plan is fulfilled and until we stand before Him, perfect and complete.

---

*Dear Father, thank You for not giving up on
me. Help me to cooperate with Your process
of fulfilling Your purpose in me. Amen.*

It's All Good

And we know that all things work together
for good to them that love God, to them who
are the called according to his purpose.
ROMANS 8:28 KJV

God can and does use all things in our lives for His good purpose. Remember Joseph in the cistern, Daniel in the lions' den, and Jesus on the cross? The Lord demonstrated His resurrection power in each of those cases. He does so in our lives as well. He brings forth beauty from ashes. What are you facing that seems impossible? What situation appears hopeless? What circumstance is overwhelming you? Believe God's promise.

Dear Lord, thank You that You work all things
together for Your good purpose. May I trust You
to fulfill Your purpose in my life. Amen.

King Forever

*You, O God, are my king from ages
past, bringing salvation to the earth.*
PSALM 74:12 NLT

Sometimes it seems like every part of our lives is affected by change. Nothing ever seems to stay the same. These changes can leave us feeling unsteady in the present and uncertain about the future. It's different in God's kingdom. He's the King now, just as He was in the days of Abraham. His reign will continue until the day His Son returns to earth and then on into eternity. We can rely—absolutely depend on—His unchanging nature. Take comfort in the stability of the King—He's our leader now and forever!

---

*Almighty King, You are my rock. When my
world is in turmoil and changes swirl around
me, You are my anchor and my center of balance.
Thank You for never changing. Amen.*

High Expectations

"They found grace out in the desert. . . . Israel,
out looking for a place to rest, met God out looking
for them!" GOD told them, "I've never quit loving you
and never will. Expect love, love, and more love!"
JEREMIAH 31:2–3 MSG

Despite their transgressions, God told the Israelites
He never quit loving them. That is true for you today.
Look beyond any circumstances and you will discover
God looking at you, His eyes filled with love. Scripture
promises an overwhelming, unexpected river of love
that will pour out when we trust the Lord our God.
Rest today in His Word. Expect God's love, love, and
more love to fill that empty place in your life.

Father, I read these words and choose this day
to believe in Your unfailing love. Amen.

He Won't Let You Down

I tell you that Christ has become a servant of the Jews on behalf of God's truth, so that the promises made to the patriarchs might be confirmed.
ROMANS 15:8 NIV

Everyone has been hurt at one time or another by a broken promise. When that happens, it is best to forgive and go on. People are just people. They mess up. But there is one who will never break His promises to us—our heavenly Father. We can safely place our hope in Him. Choose to place your hope in God's promises. You won't be discouraged by time—God's timing is always perfect. You won't be discouraged by circumstances—God can change everything in a heartbeat. He is faithful.

Lord, I choose this day to place my trust in You, for I know You're the one true constant. Amen.

Darkness into Light

*We can rejoice, too, when we run into problems and
trials, for we know that they help us develop endurance.
And endurance develops strength of character, and
character strengthens our confident hope of salvation.*
ROMANS 5:3–4 NLT

Whether it's an illness, job loss, strained friendship, or
even the everyday challenges that sneak up, we want
to find the quickest way out. Fortunately, we have a
loving God who promises to stay beside us through the
darkness. Even though night does come, the quickest
way to see the morning is to take God's hand and walk
through the hard times. In the morning, the sun rises
and the darkness fades, but God is still there. God
never promised that our lives would be easy, but He
did promise that He would always be with us—in the
darkness and all through the night.

---

*God, thank You for being a constant source of
comfort and dependability in my life. Amen.*

DAY 331
Above and Beyond

Now to him who is able to do immeasurably more than all we ask or imagine, according to his power that is at work within us, to him be glory in the church and in Christ Jesus throughout all generations, for ever and ever!
EPHESIANS 3:20–21 NIV

Think for a moment: What have you asked for? What have you imagined? It's amazing to think that God, in His infinite power and wisdom, can do immeasurably more than all that! How? According to the power that is at work within us. It's not our power, thankfully. We don't have enough power to scrape the surface of what we'd like to see done in our lives. But His power in us gets the job done. . .and more. Praise the Lord! Praise Him in the church and throughout all generations! He's an immeasurable God.

Heavenly Father, I feel pretty powerless at times. It's amazing to realize how powerful You are. Today, I praise You for going above and beyond all I could ask or imagine. Amen.

Breath of Life

He heals the brokenhearted and binds up their wounds
[healing their pain and comforting their sorrow].
PSALM 147:3 AMP

When your life brings disappointment, hurt, and pain that are almost unbearable, remember that you serve the one who heals hearts. He knows you best and loves you most. When the wind is knocked out of you and you feel like there is no oxygen left in the room, let God provide you with the air you need to breathe. Breathe out a prayer to Him, and breathe in His peace and comfort today.

Lord, be my breath of life, today and always. Amen.

Be Still and Learn

His delight and desire are in the law of the Lord,
and on His law (the precepts, the instructions,
the teachings of God) he habitually meditates
(ponders and studies) by day and by night.

PSALM 1:2 AMPC

It takes discipline to spend time with the Lord, but that
simple discipline helps to keep our hope alive, providing
light for our paths. When the schedule seems to loom
large or the weariness of everyday living tempts you
to neglect prayer and Bible study—remember they are
your lifeline. They keep you growing in your relationship
with the Lover of your soul.

Heavenly Father, I want to know You more. I want
to feel Your presence. Teach me Your ways that I
may dwell in the house of the Lord forever. Amen.

Answered Prayer

The humble shall see this, and be glad:
and your heart shall live that seek God.
PSALM 69:32 KJV

There's encouragement in answered prayer. Sometimes God's answers look exactly like what we were hoping for. Other times they reveal that God's love, wisdom, and creativity far surpass ours. To be aware of God's answers to prayer, we have to keep our eyes and hearts open. Be on the alert for answers to prayer today. When you catch sight of one, thank God. Allow the assurance of God's everlasting care to encourage your soul.

Help me to be aware of Your everyday
blessings, Lord. I want to see Your hand
in everything. Open my eyes and my heart
to receive all You have for me. Amen.

Full Redemption and Love

*Israel, put your hope in the L*ORD*, for with the L*ORD
is unfailing love and with him is full redemption.
PSALM 130:7 NIV

The Bible tells us that God removes our sins as far as the east is from the west (Psalm 103:12) and that He remembers our sin no more (Isaiah 43:25; Hebrews 8:12). It's so important to confess your sins to the Lord as soon as you feel convicted and then turn from them and move in a right direction. There is no reason to hang your head in shame over sins of the past. Don't allow the devil to speak lies into your life. You have full redemption through Jesus Christ!

Dear Jesus, I confess my sin to You. Thank You for blotting out each mistake and not holding anything against me. Help me to make right choices through the power of Your Spirit inside me. Amen.

Jonah's Prayer

*"When my life was ebbing away, I remembered you,
LORD, and my prayer rose to you, to your holy temple."*
JONAH 2:7 NIV

In verse 6 of his great prayer from the belly of the fish,
we read these words: "But you, LORD my God, brought
my life up from the pit." When Jonah reached a point
of desperation, he realized that God was his only hope.
Have you been there? Not in the belly of a great fish
but in a place where you are made keenly aware that it
is time to turn back to God? God loves His children
and always stands ready to receive us when we need a
second chance.

---

*Father, like Jonah, I sometimes think my own ways
are better than Yours. Help me to be mindful that
Your ways are always good and right. Amen.*

Put On Love

And over all these virtues put on love,
which binds them all together in perfect unity.
COLOSSIANS 3:14 NIV

There is one accessory that always fits, always looks right, always is appropriate, and always makes us more attractive to others. When we wear it, we are beautiful. When we wear it, we become more popular, more sought after, more admired. What is that accessory, you ask, and where can you buy it? It's love, and you can't buy it anywhere. But it's free, and it's always available through the Holy Spirit. When we call on Him to help us love others, He cloaks us in a beautiful covering that draws people to us and makes us perfectly lovely in every way.

Dear Father, as I get dressed each day,
help me to remember that the most important
accessory I can wear is Your love. Amen.

Loving Sisters

*But Ruth replied, "Don't urge me to leave you
or to turn back from you. Where you go I will
go, and where you stay I will stay. Your people
will be my people and your God my God."*
RUTH 1:16 NIV

The story of Ruth and Naomi is inspiring on many levels. Both women realized that their commitment, friendship, and love for each other surpassed any of their differences. They were a blessing to each other. Do you have girlfriends who would do almost anything for you? A true friendship is a gift from God. Those relationships provide us with love, companionship, encouragement, loyalty, honesty, understanding, and more! Lasting friendships are essential to living a balanced life.

---

*Father God, thank You for giving us the gift of
friendship. May I be the blessing to my girlfriends
that they are to me. Please help me to always
encourage and love them and to be a loving support
for them in both their trials and their happiness.
I praise You for my loving sisters! Amen.*

DAY 339
Open the Book

For everything that was written in the past
was written to teach us, so that through the
endurance taught in the Scriptures and the
encouragement they provide we might have hope.
ROMANS 15:4 NIV

Life is tough. We get discouraged and, at times, disheartened to the point of such despair that it's hard to recover. Reading *all* of God's Word is paramount. It is the source of hope, peace, encouragement, salvation, and so much more. It moves people to take action while diminishing depression and discouragement. As the writer of Hebrews put it, "For the word of God is alive and active. Sharper than any double-edged sword. . ." (Hebrews 4:12 NIV). Need some encouragement? Open the Book.

Lord, help me read Your Word consistently to empower
me with the hope and encouragement I need. Amen.

DAY 340
I Give Up

*God so loved the world that he gave his one
and only Son, that whoever believes in him
shall not perish but have eternal life.*
JOHN 3:16 NIV

Our Creator God cares enough about us to delve into our everyday lives and help us. Through the Holy Spirit within, God's gentle hand of direction will sustain each of us, enabling us to grow closer to our Father. The closer we grow to Him, the more like Him we desire to be. Then His influence spreads through us to others. When we surrender, He is able to use our lives and enrich others. What a powerful message: give up and give more!

---

*Lord, thank You for loving us despite our frailties.
What an encouragement to me today. Amen.*

Lord, Help!

"Lord, help!" they cried in their trouble, and he saved them from their distress. He calmed the storm to a whisper and stilled the waves. What a blessing was that stillness as he brought them safely into harbor!

PSALM 107:28–30 NLT

Samuel Morse, the father of modern communication, said, "The only gleam of hope, and I cannot underrate it, is from confidence in God. When I look upward it calms any apprehension for the future, and I seem to hear a voice saying: 'If I clothe the lilies of the field, shall I not also clothe you?' Here is my strong confidence, and I will wait patiently for the direction of Providence." The answer to your prayer does not depend on you. Your expressions of your heart spoken to your Father bring Him onto the scene for any reason you need Him.

Father, thank You for hearing my prayers. I know that You are always near to me and You answer my heart's cry. Help me to come to You first instead of trying to do things on my own. Amen.

Cartwheels of Joy

I'm singing joyful praise to GOD. I'm turning cartwheels of joy to my Savior God. Counting on GOD's Rule to prevail, I take heart and gain strength. I run like a deer. I feel like I'm king of the mountain!
HABAKKUK 3:18–19 MSG

What would happen if we followed the advice of the psalmist and turned a cartwheel of joy in our hearts—regardless of the circumstances—then leaned into and trusted His rule to prevail? Think of the happiness and peace that could be ours with a total surrender to God's care. Taking a giant step, armed with scriptures and praise and joy, we can surmount any obstacle put before us, running like a deer, climbing the tall mountains. With God at our side, it's possible to be king of the mountain.

Dear Lord, I need Your help. Gently guide me so I might learn to lean on You and become confident in Your care. Amen.

Like Little Children

One day some parents brought their children to Jesus so he could touch and bless them. But the disciples scolded the parents for bothering him. When Jesus saw what was happening, he was angry with his disciples. He said to them, "Let the children come to me. Don't stop them! For the Kingdom of God belongs to those who are like these children. I tell you the truth, anyone who doesn't receive the Kingdom of God like a child will never enter it."

MARK 10:13–15 NLT

This passage in Mark tells us that no matter how old we are, God wants us to come to Him with the faith of a child. He wants us to be open and honest about our feelings. He wants us to trust Him wholeheartedly, just like little kids do. As adults, we sometimes play games with God. We tell God what we think He wants to hear, forgetting that He already knows our hearts! God is big enough to handle your honesty. Tell Him how you really feel.

Father, help me come to You as a little child and be more open and honest with You in prayer. Amen.

DAY 344
A Prayer Away

In the day when I cried thou answeredst me,
and strengthenedst me with strength in my soul.
PSALM 138:3 KJV

A word of encouragement can go a long way in strengthening our hearts. Whether that word comes from a friend, a spouse, a stranger, or straight from God's own Word, encouragement has power. It lets us know we're not alone. We have a support group cheering us on as we go through life. Out of that support group, God is our biggest fan. He wants you to succeed, and His help is just a prayer away.

Encourage me with Your truth, Lord.
Remind me of Your love and faithfulness.
Help me live each day knowing the truth
about You and who I am in You. Amen.

Encourage One Another

*Therefore encourage one another and build each
other up, just as in fact you are doing.*
1 THESSALONIANS 5:11 NIV

Encouragement is more than words. It is also valuing,
being tolerant of, serving, and praying for one another.
It is looking for what is good and strong in a person and
celebrating it. Encouragement means sincerely forgiving
and asking for forgiveness, recognizing someone's weaknesses and holding out a helping hand, giving humbly
while building someone up, helping others to hope in
the Lord, and praying that God will encourage them in
ways that you cannot. Whom will you encourage today?

---

*Heavenly Father, open my eyes to those who need
encouragement. Show me how I can help. Amen.*

Trials and Wisdom

Consider it pure joy, my brothers and sisters, whenever you face trials of many kinds, because you know that the testing of your faith produces perseverance. Let perseverance finish its work so that you may be mature and complete, not lacking anything. If any of you lacks wisdom, you should ask God, who gives generously to all without finding fault, and it will be given to you.

JAMES 1:2–5 NIV

Things won't be easy and simple until we get to heaven. So how can we avoid becoming discouraged? We remember that God is good. We trust His faithfulness. We pray for wisdom and believe that God is working every single trial and triumph together for our good and for His glory. This passage in James tells us that when we lack wisdom, we should simply ask God for it! Be encouraged that the Lord will give you wisdom generously without finding fault!

Lord Jesus, please give me wisdom. Help me give You all my burdens and increase my faith in You. Amen.

You Are a
Woman of Worth

*A wife of noble character who can find? She is
worth far more than rubies. Her husband has full
confidence in her and lacks nothing of value. She
brings him good, not harm, all the days of her life.*

PROVERBS 31:10–12 NIV

Are you the woman of worth that Jesus intends you
to be? We often don't think we are. Between running
a household, rushing to work, taking care of the children, volunteering for worthwhile activities, and still
being a role model for our families, we think we've
failed miserably. Sometimes we don't fully realize that
learning to be a noble woman of character takes time.
Our experiences can be offered to another generation
seeking wisdom from others who have "been there."
You are a woman of worth. God said so!

---

*Father God, thank You for equipping me to
be a woman of noble character. Help me to be
the woman You intend me to be! Amen.*

DAY 348
Solid Ground

They that trust in the LORD shall be as mount Zion,
which cannot be removed, but abideth for ever.
PSALM 125:1 KJV

Alpine peaks endure sun and showers, heat and hail. They don't yield or bow to adverse conditions, but continue to stand firm, being exactly what God created them to be—majestic mountains. God created you to be a strong, victorious woman. You were designed to endure the changing seasons of this life with God's help. Lean on Him when the winds of life begin to blow. God and His Word are solid ground that will never shift beneath your feet.

When trouble comes, I won't be shaken, because
You hold me firmly in Your hand. I trust You, Lord.
You are my rock and my strong tower. Amen.

God's Promises Bring Hope

*"For I know the plans I have for you,
plans to prosper you and not to harm you,
plans to give you hope and a future."*
JEREMIAH 29:11 NIV

The writer of the well-known hymn "It Is Well with My Soul" penned those words at the most grief-stricken time of his life after his four daughters were tragically killed at sea. His undaunted faith remained because he believed in a God who was bigger than the tragedy he faced. God's promises gave him hope and encouragement. Despite your circumstances, God has a plan for you, one that will give you encouragement and hope and a brighter future.

Father, may I always say, "It is well with my soul," knowing that Your promises are true and that I can trust You no matter what. Amen.

Walk a Mile in the Master's Shoes

For this very reason also, applying all diligence, in your faith supply moral excellence, and in your moral excellence, knowledge.

2 PETER 1:5 NASB

God, in His infinite grace and mercy, knows we'll stumble. We can place our hope in Him with confidence He'll understand. He's not there with a "giant thumb" to squash us as we toddle along, new in our spiritual walk. He doesn't look for opportunities to say, "Aha, you messed up!" Quite the contrary: He encourages us with His Word. As we grow and learn with the aid of the Spirit, our lives will also reflect more of Him. And as we grow ever more sure-footed, we'll reach our destination—to be like our Father.

---

*Gracious Lord, thank You for Your
ever-present guidance. Amen.*

Linking Hearts with God

"You will receive power when the Holy
Spirit comes on you; and you will be my
witnesses. . .to the ends of the earth."
ACTS 1:8 NIV

God knows our hearts. He knows what we need to make it through a day. So in His kindness, He gave us a gift in the form of the Holy Spirit. As a counselor, a comforter, and a friend, the Holy Spirit acts as our inner compass. He upholds us when times are hard and helps us hear God's directions. When the path of obedience grows dark, the Spirit floods it with light. What revelation! He lives within us. Therefore, our prayers are lifted to the Father, to the very throne of God!

Father God, how blessed I am to come into
Your presence. Help me, Father, when I
am weak. Guide me this day. Amen.

Step by Step

*For we walk by faith, not by sight [living
our lives in a manner consistent with our
confident belief in God's promises].*
2 CORINTHIANS 5:7 AMP

The experiences and circumstances of our lives can often
lead us to lose heart. The apostle Paul exhorts us to look
away from this present world and rely on God by faith.
Webster's dictionary defines faith as a firm belief and
complete trust. Trusting, even when our faith is small,
is not an easy task. Today, grasp hold of God's Word
and feel His presence. Hold tightly and don't let your
steps falter. He is beside you and will lead you.

---

*Dear heavenly Father, today, I choose to clutch Your
hand and feel Your presence as I trudge the pathways
of my life. I trust You are by my side. Amen.*

DAY 353

One Day at a Time

A marathon runner doesn't start out running twenty-six miles. She has to start slow, remain consistent, and push herself a bit farther day by day. That's how endurance is built. The same is true in life. If what lies ahead seems overwhelming, don't panic thinking you need to tackle everything at once. Ask God to help you do what you can today. Then celebrate the progress you've made, rest, and repeat. Endurance only grows one day at a time.

Forgive me for my worries, Lord. Help me stay in the present moment. . .with You. When I'm overwhelmed, lead me to the rock that is higher than I. Amen.

His Steady Hand

The LORD makes firm the steps of the one who delights in him; though he may stumble, he will not fall, for the LORD upholds him with his hand.
PSALM 37:23–24 NIV

The Lord knows there are times when we will stumble. We may even backslide into the very activity that caused us to call on the Lord for salvation in the first place. But His Word assures us that His love is eternal and that when we cry out to Him, He will hear. Do not be discouraged about those stumbling blocks in your path, because the Lord is with you always. Scripture tells us we are in the palm of His hand. Hope is found in the Lord. He delights in us and wants the very best for us because of His perfect love.

Lord God, the cross was necessary for sinners like me. I thank You that You loved me enough to choose me and that I accepted the free gift of salvation. Amen.

DAY 355
Eternal Life

*Every day will I bless thee; and I will
praise thy name for ever and ever.*
PSALM 145:2 KJV

Eternal life isn't a reward we can earn. It's a free gift
given by a Father who wants to spend eternity with
the children He loves. This gift may be free to us, but
it was purchased at a high price. Jesus purchased our
lives at the cost of His own. His death on the cross is
the bridge that leads us from this life into the next.
Forever isn't long to say thank you for a gift like that.

---

*Jesus, help me never take your great sacrifice for
granted. I'm free because You paid dearly for my
freedom. Let me live my life in thanksgiving. Amen.*

Childlike Wonder

*Thou wilt shew me the path of life: in thy
presence is fulness of joy; at thy right hand
there are pleasures for evermore.*
PSALM 16:11 KJV

Johann Wolfgang von Goethe wrote, "Life is the child-
hood of our immortality." In light of eternity, you're just
a kid—regardless of your age. In today's youth-obsessed
society, keeping your "true" age in mind can help you see
each day from a more heavenly perspective. Hold on to
your sense of childlike wonder. Allow it to inspire awe,
thanks, praise, and delight. Draw near to your heavenly
Father and celebrate. There's so much more to your life
than meets the eye.

*Father, I ask that You give me a heavenly perspective
on this world. . .and on my life. I want to live
with the faith of a child, in awe of who You are
and what You have in store for me. Amen.*

Raise the Roof

*Come, let's shout praises to GOD, raise the roof for
the Rock who saved us! Let's march into his presence
singing praises, lifting the rafters with our hymns!*
PSALM 95:1–2 MSG

Not many had it rougher than King David, who curled
up in caves to hide from his enemies, or Paul in a dark
dungeon cell, yet they still praised God despite the
circumstances. And our God extended His grace to
them as they acclaimed Him in their suffering. The
Lord wants to hear our shouts of joy and see us march
into the courtyard rejoicing. He hears our faltering
songs and turns them into a symphony for His ears. So
lift up your voice and join in the praise to our Creator
and Lord.

---

*Dear heavenly Father, I praise Your holy
name. Bless You, Lord. Thank You for Your
grace and mercy toward me. Amen.*

DAY 358
Hope in the Alpha and Omega

"I am the First and the Last.
I am the beginning and the end."
REVELATION 22:13 NLV

Jesus says several times in the Bible that He is the first and the last, the beginning and the end. Some Bible translations use the words Alpha and Omega; those are the names of the first and last letters in the Greek alphabet. He is A and Z in our alphabet. Jesus is everything and has always existed. He has gone before us, and He goes ahead of us. He surrounds us on all sides. We struggle to wrap our minds around this truth, but we can rest in the fact that Jesus knows and always has known the whole story of our lives.

Dear Jesus, You are the beginning and
the end of all things. I am so blessed to call
You my hope and my Savior. Amen.

He Carries Us

In his love and mercy he redeemed them. He lifted
them up and carried them through all the years.
ISAIAH 63:9 NLT

Are you feeling broken today? Depressed? Defeated?
Run to Jesus and not away from Him. He will carry
us—no matter what pain we have to endure, no matter
what happens to us. God sent Jesus to be our Redeemer.
He knew the world would hate, malign, and kill Jesus.
Yet, He allowed His very flesh to writhe in agony on
the cross—so that we could also become His sons and
daughters. He loved us that much.

Lord Jesus, thank You for coming to us—for not
abandoning us when we are broken. Thank You for
Your work on the cross, for Your grace, mercy, and love.
Help me to seek You even when I can't feel You, to love
You even when I don't know all the answers. Amen.

The Gift of Encouragement

*We have different gifts. . . . If it is to
encourage, then give encouragement.*
ROMANS 12:6, 8 NIV

Paul spoke of encouragement as a God-given desire to proclaim God's Word in such a way that it touches hearts to move them to receive the gospel. Encouragement is a vital part of witnessing because encouragement is doused with God's love. For the believer, it stimulates our faith to produce a deeper commitment to Christ. It brings hope to the disheartened or defeated soul. It restores hope. How will you know your spiritual gift? Ask God and then follow the desires He places on your heart.

---

*Father, help me tune in to the needs of those around
me so that I might encourage them for the gospel's
sake for Your glory and their good. Amen.*

Building Trust

*Trust in the LORD with all your heart and lean not
on your own understanding; in all your ways submit
to him, and he will make your paths straight.*
PROVERBS 3:5–6 NIV

Placing our trust in a loving heavenly Father can sometimes feel like stepping off a precipice. Perhaps it is because we can't see God. Trust is not easily attained. It comes once you have built a record with another over a period of time. It involves letting go and knowing you will be caught. In order to trust God, we must step out in faith. Challenge yourself to trust God with one detail in your life each day. Build that trust pattern and watch Him work. He will not let you down.

*Father, I release my hold on my life
and trust in You. Amen.*

Biblical Encouragement for Your Heart

*Don't be concerned about the outward beauty of fancy
hairstyles, expensive jewelry, or beautiful clothes.
You should clothe yourselves instead with the beauty
that comes from within, the unfading beauty of a
gentle and quiet spirit, which is so precious to God.*

1 PETER 3:3–4 NLT

God is concerned with what is on the inside. He listens
to how you respond to others and watches the facial
expressions you choose to exhibit. He sees your heart.
The Lord desires that you clothe yourself with a gentle
and quiet spirit. He declares this as unfading beauty,
the inner beauty of the heart. Focus on this and no
one will even notice whether your jewelry shines. Your
face will be radiant with the joy of the Lord, and your
heart will overflow with grace and peace.

---

*Lord, grant me a quiet and gentle spirit.
I ask this in Jesus' name. Amen.*

The Gift of Prayer

First of all, then, I urge that petitions (specific requests), prayers, intercessions (prayers for others) and thanksgivings be offered on behalf of all people. . . . This [kind of praying] is good and acceptable and pleasing in the sight of God our Savior.

1 TIMOTHY 2:1, 3 AMP

There is such joy in giving gifts. Seeing the delight on someone's face to receive something unexpected is exciting. Perhaps the absolute greatest gift one person can give to another doesn't come in a box. It can't be wrapped or presented formally; instead, it is the words spoken to God for someone—the gift of prayer. When we pray for others, we ask God to intervene and to make Himself known to them. We can pray for God's plan and purpose in their lives. We can ask God to bless them or protect them. Who would God have you give the gift of prayer to today?

Lord, thank You for bringing people to my mind who need prayer. Show me how to give the gift of prayer to those You would have me pray for. Amen.

DAY 364
Ultimate Example

I will meditate in thy precepts,
and have respect unto thy ways.
PSALM 119:15 KJV

In the Bible we read about heroes such as Abraham, Moses, and David. Though these men did admirable things, they were also flawed. They made mistakes and poor choices. Nevertheless, God used them in remarkable ways. The only person in the Bible who lived a perfect life was Jesus. He is our ultimate example. If you're searching for the best way to live and love, Jesus' footsteps are the only ones wholly worth following.

Thank You for using me despite my flaws, Lord. I bring them all to You to create whatever You would make of my life. My life is Yours, God. Amen.

DAY 365

Joyous Light

Whom having not seen, ye love; in whom,
though now ye see him not, yet believing,
ye rejoice with joy unspeakable and full of glory.
1 PETER 1:8 KJV

Jesus is the light of the world. When we accept Him, the light is poured into us. The Holy Spirit comes to reside within, bringing His light—a glorious gift graciously given to us. When we realize the importance of the gift and the blessings that result from a life led by the Father, we can't contain our happiness. The joy and hope that fill our hearts well up. Joy uncontained comes when Jesus becomes our Lord. Through Him, through faith, we have hope for the future. What joy! So let it spill forth in love.

Lord, help me to be a light unto the world,
shining forth Your goodness. Amen.

Scripture Index

OLD TESTAMENT